SPORTS in the CAROLINAS
From Death Valley to Tobacco Road

SPORTS in the CAROLINAS
From Death Valley to Tobacco Road

EDITED BY ED SOUTHERN

NOVELLO FESTIVAL PRESS

CHARLOTTE, NORTH CAROLINA 2009

Sports in the Carolinas: From Death Valley to Tobacco Road
Edited by Ed Southern
Novello Festival Press, Charlotte, North Carolina

Copyright © 2009 by Ed Southern;
Please see page 154 for an extension of the copyright page
Copyrights for other contributed materials are held by the respective authors

All Rights Reserved
Published in the United States by Novello Festival Press, Charlotte, North Carolina
ISBN-13: 978-0-9815192-2-7
ISBN-10: 0-9815192-2-9
Design and composition by Jacky Woolsey, Paper Moon Graphics, Inc.
Printed in Canada

While every effort has been made to verify the accuracy of the material contained in this book, neither the publisher, editor nor authors are responsible for any errors or omissions.

Library of Congress Cataloging-in-Publication Data

Southern, Ed, 1972–
Sports in the Carolinas : from death valley to tobacco road by Ed Southern.
    p. cm.
  Includes index.
  ISBN-13: 978-0-9815192-2-7 (trade pbk.)
  ISBN-10: 0-9815192-2-9 (trade pbk.)
  1. Sports—North Carolina—History—Anecdotes. 2. Sports—South Carolina—History—Anecdotes. I. Title.
GV584.N8S68 2009
796.09756—dc22

                                         2009006330

To Jamie

Contents

INTRODUCTION ... ix

SECTION 1 THE GAMES

Highlights of Easter Monday in North Carolina
    R. G. (Hunk) Utley ... 3
The Outlaw Carolina League, 1936–1938 *R. G. (Hank) Utley* ... 5
GOLF IN PINEHURST ... 7
The East Coast Rose Bowl *Michael Scott* ... 10
A STATE DIVIDED ... 12
Nose Dive *Jack Igelman* ... 15
DID *BULL DURHAM* SAVE THE MINOR LEAGUES? ... 17
A Triumph for Title IX *Susan Shackleford* ... 19
March 2008 *Michael Kruse* ... 21

SECTION 2 THE TEAMS

The Incredible True Story of the 1951 Rocks *Matthew Musson* ... 37
THE CARDIAC PACK ... 39
Big House, Billy, and the Unofficial Integration
    of Winston-Salem *Clarence E. Gaines with Clint Johnson* ... 42
THE CHARLOTTE HORNETS ... 46
Mountaineers Bring Down the Big House *Dick Brown* ... 49
"THE GREATEST COLLEGE SPORTS PROGRAM EVER" ... 54
Proud To Be a Deacon *Ed Southern* ... 56

	Carolina Panthers	61
	Carolina Hurricanes	64
SECTION 3	**THE PLAYERS**	
	An Elegy for Ernie Shore *Ed Southern*	69
	Shoeless Joe Jackson	71
	Choo Choo *Ron Green, Sr.*	73
	Junior Johnson	76
	Synchronized Swim *Betty Brown*	78
	Arnold Palmer	80
	Mary Garber Stood Very Tall in a Man's World *Lenox Rawlings*	81
	David Thompson	85
	The World's Number One, Flat-Out, All-Time Great Driver: Richard Petty *Jerry Bledsoe*	88
	Joe Frazier	99
	"A Limousine Riding, Jet Flying, Kiss Stealing, Wheeling and Dealing Son of a Gun" *Tom Sorensen*	102
	"Sweet D" *David Dickson*	105
	Dale Earnhardt: The Man in Black *Sharyn McCrumb*	107
	Michael Jordan	113
	A Special Athlete *Ann Campanella*	116
	Ryan Newman's Canine Connection *Kris Johnson*	118
SECTION 4	**THE COACHES**	
	The Coach in the Basement *Will Blythe*	123
	Danny Ford: The Man, the God *Michel S. Stone*	132
	Coach K *Jim Sumner*	135
	Born to Coach, Summerville Legend John McKissick Not About to Stop *Rob Young*	141
	"When Life Kicks You, Let It Kick You Forward: The Life and Impact of Kay Yow *Susan Shackleford*	144
	Acknowledgments	149
	List of Contributors	151
	Credits	154
	Index	155

Introduction

January 28, 2009
6:00 PM

If you think I'm a nervous wreck now, wait until the game starts.

In 60 minutes, "my" team, the Wake Forest Demon Deacons, will play the #1-ranked Duke Blue Devils in a nationally televised college basketball game. I will not play in this game; I will not even be at this game. Yet I'm jittery, anxious, and distracted.

Why does this mean so much to me, how well a collection of college kids may or may not put a leather ball through an iron hoop?

Why do so many people care so much about the games they watch or play?

This book does not make a full attempt to answer that question. That would take an expertise in psychology, anthropology, and history that neither I nor any of the contributors possess. This book does look at that question, though, through the stories inside—stories that reveal the depth of people's devotion to sports, and the impact that sports can have on not only those who play and watch, but on everybody who lives in the Carolinas.

When Amy Rogers at Novello Festival Press asked me to edit this anthology, I said yes without hesitation or reflection. I jumped at the opportunity; it was a no-brainer. Then my brain started to reflect a bit on sports in the Carolinas, and I realized what I had gotten myself into. The Carolinas are so rich in sports, in great teams and athletes, in legendary coaches, that including them all would produce not a book, but a set of encyclopedias. I could fill a book just listing all the all-time greats with a connection to the Carolinas. If your favorite sports figures or stories aren't featured in this book, don't think of them as having been cut; think of them as being saved for a possible sequel (was Bob Knight the coach who said, "We didn't lose, we just ran out of time"?).

The Carolinas haven't just produced so many who played or coached their games extremely well; the Carolinas have produced more than their share of individuals who have changed their games, and sometimes society as a whole, forever. The Carolinas can justifiably claim to have created a large portion of the modern world of sports. Can you imagine the NBA if Michael Jordan had never played? Can you imagine the game of basketball itself without John McLendon, who invented the fast break at what is now North Carolina Central University? Would March Madness be quite as mad without Dean Smith, Jim Valvano, Mike Krzyzewski, and the teams they coached?

The U.S. Women's Soccer team would probably not have captured their World Cups, much less America's fascination, without Anson Dorrance and his UNC program. Women wouldn't have much opportunity to play sports at all without the late Kay Yow, nor would they have much opportunity to cover sports as reporters without the late Mary Garber. Tiger Woods would not be the world's richest athlete if Arnold Palmer had never honed his golf game in the Carolinas. NASCAR, if it had survived at all, would be a low-budget regional pastime without Junior Johnson, Richard Petty, and Dale Earnhardt. Heck, Kevin Costner wouldn't have much of an acting career without the Durham Bulls and "Shoeless" Joe Jackson.

Those men and women are all featured in this book, along with many others. Rob Young writes about John McKissick, the record-setting high school football coach in Summerville, South Carolina. Michel Stone writes about her childhood crush on Clemson head football coach Danny Ford. Michael Scott writes about the only Rose Bowl ever played on the East Coast. Ron Green, Sr., writes about Charlie "Choo Choo" Justice, who twice was runner-up for the Heisman Trophy. Ann Campanella writes about watching her brother compete in the Special Olympics World Games. Betty Brown shares a light-hearted look at her time on the Queens College synchronized swim team in the 1950s. Tom Sorensen gives some insight into the person renowned worldwide as the Nature Boy, Ric Flair.

This book could not include every sport played by Carolinians, or every Carolinian who competed at the highest levels of their sports, but it does give an entertaining look at sports as they're played and followed in the Carolinas.

10:00 PM

Wake Forest's James Johnson hit a layup with less than a second left to beat Duke by two points. I am no longer a nervous wreck. Now I'm exhausted. My throat is sore, my neighbors probably want me evicted. Why do I do this to myself?

Wake Forest, Duke, and all other colleges and universities were founded to educate people, not field basketball teams. Though my school has a sterling academic reputation, I do not wake up eager to check the *U.S. News & World Report* rankings like I do the latest Associated Press polls, and to my knowledge there are no websites devoted to talking trash about comparative SAT scores (and I sure hope there aren't). The great Paul "Bear" Bryant said, "It's kind of hard to rally 'round a math class," and it's so self-evidently true that very few people would argue—and, even though math is vastly more important to quality of life, those few would be dismissed as crackpots.

W. H. Auden said of music that "every high C accurately struck utterly demolishes the theory that we are the irresponsible puppets of fate or chance." If I were that smart, I would say the same about Jordan's jump shot to win the 1982 NCAA championship, or Palmer knocking the ball between the pines at Augusta National, or Earnhardt's "pass in the grass." Though no one ever says, "That was a baseball game of a ballet" (though they often say the reverse), great sports contain much of what we appreciate and enjoy about great art: rigorous discipline, wondrous natural talent, extensive preparation, single-minded devotion, sudden inspiration and the confidence to act on it, thrills, chills, surprises. Like art, sports point us toward the full potential of human beings; no one would have thought the ceiling of the Sistine Chapel possible until Michelangelo did it, and no one thought a sub-four-minute mile possible until Roger Bannister did it. For that matter, few people thought African-Americans could compete on an equal level with whites until Jackie Robinson did it.

Unlike art, sports include the great joy of direct confrontation and clear winners. We cannot say with absolute certainty that William Faulkner is a greater novelist than Ernest Hemingway, the way we can that Wake Forest's men's basketball team beat Duke's tonight. We may not be proud of it, but confrontation and competition are fundamentals of human nature; better that we get those out of our system on the field or the court (or in the stands or in front of the television) than on the battlefield or the duelists' field of honor.

Sports teams stand in for our hometowns, our home states, our schools; the players are the champions we send forward to represent us. We are convinced, as our new president is, that the way people play their chosen games says something about their character—and, vicariously, about ours. That makes no sense in any analysis, but we sense an instinctive rightness about it.

That's what the love of sports comes down to, whether you are watching or playing: the sense of it, the enjoyment of it, the sheer fun of it. It's fun to try to hit, catch, or throw a ball; to try to score a goal, or keep your opponent from scoring one; to win fair and square. It's fun to watch someone else do those things far better than most of us ever could. It's fun to share in the traditions, the rituals, the excitement of watching a story happen right in front of you in real time, not knowing how or even, sometimes, when it's going to end.

And it's fun—even enlightening on occasion—to re-tell those stories, and relive the things about them that meant so much.

—Ed Southern

1
THE GAMES

Highlights of Easter Monday in North Carolina

By R. G. (Hank) Utley

On April 3, 1899, North Carolina A&M (now North Carolina State University) hosted Mebane Military School in the first of 58 consecutive Easter Monday baseball games. Mebane defeated A&M, 5–4, in 11 innings. The *Raleigh News & Observer* noted that 700 fans attended the game, "christening the new A&M Diamond, with a large number of ladies present."

Easter Monday has been a traditional holiday for centuries. Many churches in Eastern Europe still celebrate the end of Lent (40 days of fasting and penitence) with large family, neighborhood and church socials.

From 1899, Easter Monday developed into the greatest social event in North Carolina. The three girls' colleges in Raleigh (Peace, St. Mary's, and Baptist Female University, now Meredith College) helped make it an outstanding Easter Parade, leading all the females in the area to wear Easter hats, dresses and corsages to the ballgame. The North Carolina Legislature began adjourning so members could attend the game in their special carriages and/or automobiles.

On April 8, 1901, Wake Forest College (then located in Wake County) brought many students to Raleigh to see Wake Forest defeat A&M, 12–6. The newspaper report stated, "extremely large crowd present, in it being many ladies and among these, the students from the various female schools in Raleigh, an Easter Parade."

In 1906 two significant events added to the social luster of the Easter Monday baseball game. Trinity College (now Duke University) defeated A&M, and the social pages reported two automobile parties from Durham drove the dusty roads to the game, played at the Raleigh Fairgrounds. One thousand five hundred fans attended. Among those riding those dusty roads were Mr. A.B. Duke and Mr. George Lyon, driving two cars with guests from New York City, Yale University, Durham, and Henderson, North Carolina.

That night, April 16, 1906, the Alpha Epsilon Chapter of Pi Kappa Alpha at A&M hosted the first of more than 50 consecutive Easter Monday Dances—the "Pika Ball." In future years, North Carolina governors attended the dance and the social pages in the local paper reported names of girls attending with their dates.

By 1907 the Seaboard Railroad was running newspaper ads about special excursion round-trip trains from Henderson, Franklinton, Louisburg, Wake Forest, Norlina, and Oxford to Raleigh.

On April 5, 1915, more than 10 inches of snow was scraped from the field and the game was played because of special trains bringing in hundreds of fans, including nearly the entire Wake Forest student body shouting, "On to Raleigh."

Rain delayed many games. On March 28, 1921, after only one-third of an inning, the game was called because of rain. One week later on Monday, April 3, the game ended in a 3–3, 12-inning tie, called because of darkness. On April 4, Wake Forest won 1–0 after 11 innings. The game covered 9 days and 23–1/3 innings. The news report on the original rainout stated, "The downpour became so furious that no tradition, even one which had survived snow and sundry other rains, could defy it."

In 1923 the Pika Ball had more than 4,000 in attendance. The Pika Ball spawned a post-Easter Mardi Gras with Raleigh social clubs, the Capitol Club, Sphinx Club, Black Cat Club, Nine O'Clock Cotillion Club, and the Circle Club all having socials and/or dances following Easter Monday.

More than 6,000 fans attended the April 21, 1924, game, with N.C. State beating Wake Forest, 4–1.

As a result of pressure from all state government employees, the North Carolina General Assembly, on April 19, 1935 (Good Friday), passed a law that made the following Easter Monday, April 22, a legal North Carolina holiday for all banks and businesses. Now everyone could go to the fabled Easter Monday baseball game.

N.C. State hosted 58 Easter Monday games between 1899 and 1956. The crowds began to dwindle during the later 1940s with college boys and girls going to beaches and other locations. By 1956 Wake Forest had moved to Winston-Salem.

The legal Easter Monday holiday continued through April 20, 1987.

On March 31, 1988, several days before Easter Monday (April 4, 1988), Lew Powell, staff writer for the *Charlotte Observer*, wrote, "the holiday that baseball birthed, banks have buried."

He was referring to the North Carolina banks putting pressure on the North Carolina Legislature to change the state holiday from Easter Monday to Good Friday, thereby joining the rest of the banks in the U.S. and not losing more than one day's business. It was on August 14, 1987, that the legislature changed the state holiday to Good Friday, effective in 1988.

The Easter Monday baseball game had ceased back in 1957. Thad Eure, North Carolina Secretary of State, said, "The game was one of the biggest athletic events in the state. It was like college football and basketball are today. The railroads even ran excursion trains to Raleigh."

The Outlaw Carolina League, 1936–1938

By R. G. (Hank) Utley

In the Depression-era mill towns of the North Carolina Piedmont, a feisty professional baseball league was born. Ignoring the professional contract and reserve clause of the National Association of Professional Baseball Leagues (NAPBL), the Carolina League offered players control of their own careers. With better pay than a player could earn elsewhere and the guarantee of off-season jobs in the textile mills that supported the teams (more than 20% of the nation was unemployed), the league attracted a flock of talented players. Although done in by internal squabbling as well as opposition from organized baseball, it thrived for three unforgettable seasons, 1936–1938.

Thus, on May 18, 1936, Jake Wade, award-winning sports editor of the *Charlotte Observer*, wrote:

> "Today is opening day, you know. It's a new baseball picture for Charlotte and this section. Not organized professional baseball . . . but something which may prove just as entertaining and diverting. Certainly, it's a noble experiment, and most engaging.
>
> "Charlotte is in the Carolina League. The league abides by the rules and general plan of organized professional baseball. The ball they hit is standard and bears the league president's signature. The carefully chosen umpires are uniformed, draw regular salaries, work under strict supervision. The only difference is the players are not strictly chattels as in organized professional baseball. They can leave on a moment's notice and go to an organized professional league, but they cannot jump from one club to another in this circuit."

On June 16, 1936, a report appeared in *The Concord Tribune* that baseball players were openly jumping contracts with organized professional teams to play in the Carolina League—and that organized baseball, based in nearby Durham, was keeping track of them. The article was couched as a warning from Judge W. G. Bramham, president of the National Association of Professional Baseball:

> "Presence of players on the ineligible list of organized baseball on the rosters of clubs in the Carolina League, an independent organization, has brought forth a warning from President W.G. Bramham calling attention of all players and clubs in the National Association to conditions which exist in this outlaw league.
>
> "Judge Bramham said, 'The Carolina League, composed of Concord, Kannapolis, Salisbury, Shelby, Hickory, Forest City, Charlotte, and Valdese, is harboring and playing players under contract or reserved with organized ball. All such players are placed on the ineligible list, and all players and clubs

in organized ball are notified that the playing with or against ineligibles, or with or against clubs playing or harboring ineligible players, will bring about the ineligibility of any and all players who fail to observe this warning.'"

On December 7, 1936, after the Carolina League had completed its first season successfully, a news dispatch from the NAPBL's annual winter meetings in Montreal, Quebec, indicated that the league was the subject of much discussion, both formal and informal. The dispatch that appeared in the *Concord Tribune* quoted a minor league executive who described the Carolina League as a "haven for dissatisfied professional ball players."

After jumping a contract in organized baseball, pitcher Bud Shaney won 17 games in a row for the 1936 outlaw Charlotte Hornets. He used baseballs with phonograph needles embedded in the seams. When asked to let the umpires examine a baseball, he would throw it over the grandstand.

Edwin Collins "Alabama" Pitts received a pardon from Sing Sing Prison in New York in 1935. Because he was a felon, he was refused permission to play organized baseball. He also signed with the Hornets. After playing with Charlotte, Gastonia, and Valdese, Pitts died on June 7, 1941, in Valdese, as a result of a stabbing he received in a dance hall fight.

Vince Barton hit 16 home runs in just 102 games for the Chicago Cubs in 1931 and 1932. A heavy drinker and womanizer, he ended up back in the minor leagues. He signed with the outlaw Kannapolis Towelers in 1936. His drinking and womanizing did not prevent him from hitting five home runs in one game for the 1938 outlaw Hickory Rebels.

Tracey Hitchner refused a cut in salary from Albany, N.Y. (International League) in 1936 and signed with the Hickory Rebels in the outlaw league. After being suspended for jumping a contract in organized ball, Hitchner changed his name to John Davis in 1937. He was suspended again. In 1938 he pitched under his original name, settled down in Hickory, married a local girl and became an executive in a local furniture manufacturer.

College players made good money in the Carolina League. They did not lose their amateur standing because they had not signed a contract with professional organized baseball.

After his junior year at Duke University, Eric Tipton, All-American football and baseball star, played for the Kannapolis Towelers in 1938. He led the league in hitting with a .375 average. He signed with the Philadelphia Athletics in 1939 and played in the majors through 1945.

Richard Broadus Culler, a student-athlete at High Point University, played for the Concord Weavers from 1936–1938. Later he played his way through the minors and had a major league career from 1943–1949 with the Chicago White Sox, Boston Braves, Chicago Cubs, and New York Giants.

Lawrence "Crash" Davis played for Gastonia in 1937 after his freshman year at Duke. He hit .267. After graduating he played for the Philadelphia Athletics from 1940–1942.

George Barley pitched at Duke while under contract to the New York Yankees—a college outlaw. He pitched for the Kannapolis Towelers in 1936. After graduating, he played for Yankee farm teams from 1937–1941.

Golf in Pinehurst

James Tufts tried to provide for his guests' every need. He built them an inn, cottages, and an auditorium—an entire lovely New England-style enclave in North Carolina, laid out around a village green. He served healthy meals. He staged theatrical productions and sponsored religious services. He offered horseback riding, croquet, tennis, shooting and archery.

One day in 1897, however, he noticed a group of guests at impromptu play in a dairy field, using sticks to whack little balls at flagpoles. Tufts' reaction wasn't recorded. Chances are, he rubbed his bearded chin.

Tufts was a Boston-area apothecary who built and marketed the Arctic Soda Water Apparatus, a marble-fronted, silver-plated device for dispensing fountain drinks. Installed at food counters across America, it made him rich. In poor physical condition himself, he decided to establish a health resort as a philanthropic venture. Friends enlightened him to the North Carolina Pine Barrens, which offered scented air, cheap land free of stagnant water, and rail access to the Northeast. In 1895, he began purchasing what would become a 5,000-plus-acre tract in Moore County. Thankfully, he rejected the names Sunalia and Pinalia and settled on Pinehurst.

By early 1898, a doctor and Pinehurst patron laid out for Tufts nine golf holes ranging from 116 to 496 yards. The course proved so popular that the resort added a two-story clubhouse the following year, then nine more holes in 1900. Taking note of the physical and moral—and financial—benefits of the game, Tufts decided to hire a professional.

Enter Donald Ross.

Born in Dornoch in northern Scotland in 1872, Ross was the son of the town drunk. A mediocre student, he was once suspended from school for dunking a young lady's pigtails in an inkwell. His teacher smacked him so hard that for the rest of his life he couldn't breathe properly through one nostril. Maybe the unspoken message was that he should be more imaginative in his pranks and in his future endeavors. If so, he paid heed.

Ross grew up caddying at Royal Dornoch, Scotland's third-oldest golf club. He also played the game and learned greenskeeping and club making. In 1893, he went to St. Andrews to apprentice as greenskeeper under golf pioneer Old Tom Morris. The following year, he was hired back at Royal Dornoch. There in 1898, he met Robert Willson, an astronomy professor at Harvard, who invited him to bring his trade to the States. In March 1899, Ross did exactly that. After paying his ocean passage and then the train fare from New York to Boston, he had two dollars in his pocket. He phoned Willson, who agreed to put him up. Ross had to haul his suitcase and bag of golf clubs the four miles to Cambridge.

Tufts, hearing from friends about Ross's work at Oakley Country Club in Massachusetts, hired him at Pinehurst, initially for the winters only. The Scotsman's duties included making clubs, stocking the pro shop, managing the caddies and running the club. They soon expanded to course design, construction and maintenance. He lived, at first, in a room above a department store downtown.

Pinehurst's sandy soil was ill-suited to golf courses and most everything else. Tufts' grandson said it was so arid "that when a man was buried it was necessary to plant commercial fertilizer under him in order to afford some prospect of his being able to rise on the Day of Judgment." The resort hired the landscape architecture firm of Frederick Law Olmsted to sow nearly a quarter-million seedlings—pines, magnolias, pin oaks, holly, dogwoods, azaleas, crape myrtles and fruit trees.

Ross built his most famous Pinehurst course, No. 2, in piecemeal fashion between 1901 and 1907, the early work without drawings or plans. Thirteen holes remain mostly intact today; others were plowed under or eventually incorporated into the No. 4 course. Though he is noted for his "turtleback" greens, those were later modifications. The original putting surfaces were oiled sand. Caddies used mats to drag them smooth after each group played.

The highly challenging No. 2 was a hit among golfers. Yet many resort guests wanted relaxation, not torture. Three years later, an easier No. 3 course—since heavily rebuilt and partly absorbed into the modern No. 5 course—was completed. The more holes Ross and Pinehurst provided, the more the public wanted. By 1923, the resort had four 18-hole courses, all bearing Ross's imprint.

Pinehurst excelled at marketing. From billing itself as "America's St. Andrews" early on, it quickly became the point of comparison, courses in California and elsewhere claiming to be such things as "the Pinehurst of the Pacific." The resort held a moonlight golf contest and welcomed such stars as U.S. Open champion Francis Ouimet, who lost a featured match against Ross. It was the site of the prestigious North and South Open from 1902 to 1951. In 1936, it hosted its first major, the PGA Championship, won by Denny Shute. In 1951, it was the site of the Ryder Cup. More recently, No. 2 broke the hearts of top pros in the 1999 U.S. Open, won by popular, tam-o'-shanter–wearing Payne Stewart four months before his death in an air accident; and the 2005 U.S. Open, won by New Zealand's Michael Campbell. It is scheduled to host that tournament again in 2014.

Area golf has grown far beyond the Pinehurst Resort. Moore County boasts 40-plus courses and 150-plus miles of fairways. Some courses are famous in their own right. Pine Needles Golf Club in Southern Pines, also designed by Ross, has hosted the U.S. Women's Open multiple times. But the Pinehurst Resort remains king. It now encompasses eight courses and a trio of hotels. Its power is such that, in the late 1990s, it threatened trademark infringement suits against local businesses—businesses in the town of Pinehurst, no less—using Pinehurst in their names.

Donald Ross died in 1948 while completing his design for the Raleigh Country Club. During his playing career, he won three North and South Opens and finished fifth in the 1903 U.S. Open and eighth in the 1910 British Open. But he is best known as the first name in American course design. Besides Pinehurst No. 2, his pantheon includes Oakland Hills Country Club in Michigan and the Seminole Golf Club in Florida.

Ross christened his Pinehurst home Dornoch Cottage. Back in Scotland, however, he remained a boy from a low family who abandoned his town. Dornoch didn't even hang a plaque for him until more than a half-century after his death. Luckily, he was better appreciated in America. Warren G. Harding once gave him a signed photograph reading, "To Donald J. Ross, with tribute to a great golpher." And yes, the president caught his mistake and fixed the spelling.

—Stephen Kirk

The East Coast Rose Bowl

By Michael Scott

Duke University, in Durham, North Carolina, is not known these days for its football prowess. Far from it. But a lifetime ago, before World War II, when the helmets were made of leather, the Blue Devils were a college football powerhouse, good enough to go to the Rose Bowl in 1939. Good enough, in fact, that, a few years later, the Rose Bowl came to Duke.

The story of Duke's glory days on the football field begins in 1930, when Wallace Wade, soon after winning his third national championship as head coach of the University of Alabama Crimson Tide, announced he was leaving Tuscaloosa to coach the Blue Devils. Under Coach Wade, Duke would win five Southern Conference (the precursor to the Atlantic Coast Conference) titles in the 1930s.

The 1938 Duke team is remembered as the apogee in the school's history. This group of Blue Devils would become known as the Iron Dukes, a testament to their hard-nosed defense, and a moniker that lives today for the university's hardiest athletic boosters. The Iron Dukes were one of only three teams in major college football history to go unbeaten, untied, *and unscored upon* in the regular season. Their only blemish was a tough 7–3 loss in the Rose Bowl to the University of Southern California.

In 1941, the Duke Blue Devils were once again conference champions, sporting an undefeated record and a #2 ranking in the polls. Meanwhile, out west, the 7–2 Oregon State Beavers were winning the Pacific Coast Conference championship, earning their first-ever trip to the Rose Bowl, the oldest and most prestigious of all bowl games. In early December, Oregon State invited Duke to be their Rose Bowl opponent, and Coach Wade and his Blue Devils began preparing for the long, exciting trip to sunny southern California to cap their successful season.

Less than a week later, a Day of Infamy changed everything. After the Japanese attack at Pearl Harbor, Americans on the west coast were in a state of near-panic and constant agitation that another attack was imminent. The Army ordered that the Rose Bowl festivities be canceled, figuring a packed stadium made too enticing a target. Oregon State, not wanting to miss its first Rose Bowl, instead fielded offers to move the game, including one from Duke to host the game in North Carolina.

The Game

On New Year's Day 1942, the Rose Bowl was transplanted to the east coast for the first and last time, kicking off in Durham at the football stadium that would eventually bear Wallace Wade's name. Temporary stands—some on loan from the rival University of North Carolina Tar Heels—were added to the south end of the stadium, the open end of the horseshoe, increasing capacity from 35,000 to 55,000.

Both teams had stalwart defenses, each pitching five shut-outs during the season, but the Devils also featured a potent offense, outscoring their opponents by an average of more than 30 points. Led by quarterback Tommy Prothro (who would coincidentally go on to be head coach at Oregon State), and with home-field advantage, Duke was heavily favored, by up to two touchdowns.

But in a steady drizzle more reminiscent of the Oregon coast than the Piedmont, the Blue Devils fumbled away the opening kickoff. The teams traded touchdowns in the first half, and then again in the third quarter, making the score 14–14. Then the Beavers took the lead again, and for good this time, with a 68-yard bomb from Beaver quarterback Bob Dethman to Gene Gray. All Duke could muster in the final quarter was a safety, for a final score of 20–16, a huge upset win for Oregon State.

Duke's Coach Wade blamed himself for focusing too much on preparations for the event, and not enough on preparations for the game itself. The Devils also hurt themselves by taking leave over the Christmas holiday, a concession from Coach Wade to assuage his players for losing a much-anticipated trip to Pasadena. Neither excuse was perhaps as formidable, however, as the Oregon State defense. For both teams, the Rose Bowl was their toughest game, against their best opponent that season.

Postscript

The far-from-home Rose Bowl of 1942 presaged the upheaval facing so much of America. The game was played amid the somber mood of the nation, as it prepared to go to war in the aftermath of Pearl Harbor, not unlike the more recent days America faced following the 9/11 terrorist attacks. Most of the players, and some of the coaches, would trade uniforms soon thereafter, moving from benign gridiron battles to the worldwide theaters of the American war effort. There would be tougher battles ahead, in far less hospitable locales than Durham.

Coach Wade, who was an Army captain in the Great War—as World War I was called at the time—re-enlisted and led an artillery unit in Europe. During the Battle of the Bulge, Wade stumbled across a soldier making coffee and asked for a cup. The soldier also rustled up some food, and as the two huddled together for warmth, Wade discovered that the soldier was Stan Czech, one of the Oregon State players from that 1942 Rose Bowl.

A similar, more profound coincidence occurred in Italy, as Duke's Charlie Haynes and Oregon State's Frank Parker found themselves assigned to the same job for different companies in the same battalion. When Haynes was wounded, a chest wound so severe that Haynes said he could have fit his fist in it, during a battle near the Arno River in 1944, Parker helped carry him to safety and medical treatment. Parker recalled, "He probably would have bled to death if we hadn't gotten him to the aid station."

Four players from the 1942 Rose Bowl were killed in the war. Oregon State back Everett Smith drowned during a landing in the South Pacific. Duke's Walter

Griffith also perished in the Pacific theater. Duke running back Al Hoover smothered a Japanese hand grenade in the Battle of Peleliu Island, and Duke's star tackle Bob Nanni was killed at Iwo Jima.

A State Divided

They say that Ohio State vs. Michigan is the biggest rivalry in college sports.

"They" being people who ain't from here.

Ohio State vs. Michigan, like the Yankees vs. the Red Sox, may get more national media attention than any other rivalry in sports; Duke vs. UNC in basketball may be played for higher stakes year-in and year-out. For sheer, unbridled passion, though, no contest in the country tops the annual Battle of the Palmetto State played between the football teams of Clemson and the University of South Carolina.

This is a rivalry whose sixth game, in 1902, resulted in a full-scale riot that lasted for days. Clemson vs. USC is the longest uninterrupted rivalry in the South, the third-longest in the country. The 2004 game ended in a brawl between the players, which cost both teams their post-season berths when the coaches refused bowl bids to punish their players. The state that fired the first shots of the Civil War, the state whose politics are as solidly dominated by Republicans as they once were by Democrats, is split nearly down the middle by love or hate for the Gamecocks and the Tigers.

Given the history and the circumstances, what is most remarkable isn't the intensity of the rivalry, but the fact that so many South Carolinians whose blood runs either orange or garnet manage to get along with, even become close friends with, their neighbors on the other side—at least for the other 364 days a year.

Most states—like Ohio and Michigan—are dominated by the fan base of one major college. Others, such as North Carolina, are divided up among three or more top-level college athletic programs. In South Carolina, only Clemson and USC play in the NCAA's top division. While colleges such as Furman University and The Citadel have plenty of devoted students, alumni, and fans, Clemson and USC have more than 45,000 students currently enrolled, and hundreds of thousands of graduates and supporters throughout the state.

Clemson's Memorial Stadium, known as "Death Valley," has an official capacity of 80,301, though some games have seen crowds topping 86,000. Though a founding member of the Atlantic Coast Conference, Clemson on a game day more closely resembles a Southeastern Conference school, with traffic backing up for miles of Upstate countryside, and fans tailgating sometimes for days ahead of kickoff. The town of Clemson has a population just shy of 12,000, but it becomes the "third largest city" in the state when the Tigers play a home game.

At South Carolina, which is in the SEC, Williams-Brice Stadium holds 80,250, at least according to the fire marshal, but it has hosted overflow crowds so raucous that the concrete stands have been known to sway. In 2001, the broadcasters covering a USC-Florida game said on-air that they had to shout to hear each other over the crowd noise; in 2005, secsports.com named the game day atmosphere at Williams-Brice the best in the SEC, topping the antics in Baton Rouge, Oxford, Gainesville, and Tuscaloosa.

The animosity between the schools goes back to long before their home fields were built. It goes back to before football was even played in the state; in fact, it goes back to before Clemson University even existed. Agricultural education was one of Governor "Pitchfork" Ben Tillman's many populist causes. After first trying to gain the subject greater emphasis at South Carolina College (the forerunner of USC), Tillman seized on Thomas Clemson's bequest of his Pickens County estate to start a separate state college. The campaign to create what would become Clemson pitted Tillman against the conservatives who held much of the power among South Carolina Democrats, including some of Thomas Clemson's own relatives and Senator Wade Hampton, a Confederate hero.

More than the usual resentment between "snob schools" and "cow colleges," the antagonism between the two schools was a key battleground and symbol of a very real power struggle in South Carolina politics. In a South not far removed from the Civil War and Reconstruction, it was only a matter of time before the clash was played out on that great war-zone-by-proxy, the football field.

The first USC-Clemson game was played in 1896, during Clemson's first season of football, on a Thursday during the State Fair in Columbia. The 1902 riots kept the rivals from scheduling each other again until 1909, and the game has been played every year since, despite more than a few tense moments (and I don't mean last-minute goal line stands). In 1946, governor-elect Strom Thurmond and U.S. Secretary of State James Byrnes had to quiet a crowd ready to explode after a Clemson student strangled a live chicken during halftime. In 1961, some USC fraternity boys, dressed as Clemson players, ran onto the field before the actual team did, and proceeded to perform the usual pre-game warm-ups—very, very poorly. A number of Clemson fans, realizing the trick, managed to get onto the field and chase after the students before security guards caught them and order was restored. The 2004 game ended in an ugly brawl (is there a pretty brawl?) between the players, causing both Clemson's Tommy Bowden and Carolina's Lou Holtz to refuse post-season bowl bids as a punishment for their players.

In the game itself, Clemson leads the series 65–37–4. They also hold the edge in national championships, having been crowned in 1981. USC holds the edge in Heisman Trophy winners thanks to George Rogers, even though John Heisman himself was the Clemson coach at the turn of the 20th century. Neither team has ever dominated the series for an extended period, and both teams have pulled off upsets when the other was higher-ranked. Only one quarterback, Clemson's Charlie Whitehurst, has ever won all four Battles of the Palmetto State in which he played. This evenness keeps the rivalry hot through the ups-and-downs of the two programs; neither has ever been able to take the on-field results for granted. Since the NCAA lets its top-tier rankings be decided by polls and computers, and since the Clemson-USC game is always the last of the regular season for both schools, the game is for more than bragging rights: final standings and bowl bids usually rest on the outcome.

Even if they didn't, even if the game were played only for bragging rights, the Battle for the Palmetto State would still be . . . well, a battle, at least on the field. Let's hope that from now on it stays a neighborly disagreement off the field.

—Ed Southern

Nose Dive

By Jack Igelman

On a chilly December day more than 40 years ago, Steve Longenecker, Bob Watts and Bob Gillespie became the first rock climbers to reach the top of Looking Glass Rock in the Pisgah National Forest near Brevard, North Carolina.

Initially, the three aimed to complete a route known as the Womb on the dome's north side. But after flailing there awhile, they pointed their pitons at a considerable span of exposed granite facing northeast, in the direction of the Blue Ridge Parkway.

Before they took that stab at history, though, they studied the route with all the focus of a team of G-men. Besides buzzing frighteningly close to the cliff in a Cessna, the climbers kept vigil on the Parkway during a rainstorm to gauge the steepness of the face and determine whether any overhangs lurked above. After succeeding on a short portion at the base of the route on numerous occasions, the trio determined to finish the 450-foot vertical climb, which they did on December 17, 1966.

"The day was pretty gray with some globs of snow on the face," recalls Longenecker. "Why we chose that Sunday I'm not sure."

Four decades later, the men's route—now known as the Nose—has arguably been covered by more climbers than any other in North Carolina. At the time they completed it, though, they weren't aware of the significance of their accomplishment.

"We never thought it would be important," says Longenecker. "It was to us, of course, but we had no idea it would become so popular."

Their achievement is indisputable, especially since they completed a rather difficult climb using crude gear and clunky hiking boots at a time when there were few climbers in the South. Yet, more than 40 years later, not everyone is celebrating the accomplishment, including Longenecker.

From select overlooks along the Parkway, Looking Glass—an aged glob of hardened lava—looks like an enormous forehead bulging from the forest, its timbered hairline receding slightly. On a clear day, it's possible to visually follow a faded line up the face—the very route the three men pioneered in the '60s. So many have climbed it since that a path has been etched into the rock. Most climbers seem to accept this undeniable impact, but what many others, including Longenecker, find hard to swallow are the conditions now found at the base of the Nose.

Originally published in *Mountain XPress,* October 4, 2006.

"It's disgusting," says climber Harrison Shull, a climbing photographer and North Carolina climbing guidebook author. "The Nose area is a poster child for what we don't want a climbing site to look like."

In 1966, only a Jeep track came near the rock's base, and a thick canopy of woods pressed up against the beginning of the route. Since then, the gently graded Sun Wall Trail has channeled a steady tide of recreational climbers, school groups, wilderness programs and camps to the Nose and other popular climbs nearby. After so many years of foot traffic, the long, narrow section at the bottom is now devoid of growth, and layers of topsoil have been swept away, making the base the climbing equivalent of a superhighway.

"The climb is three or four feet longer than it once was," says Longenecker, referring to the amount of trodden soil that has washed away from the base. He admits to feeling a measure of responsibility for the current conditions.

"Back then, we never thought hammering a piton in the rock was a big deal," he says. "Other people made us aware that there's a cleaner way to climb. On the same note, climbers and programs [now] are much more aware of how things are done at the bottom."

Though the sport's degree of stewardship has evolved since the 1960s, it may not have materialized in time for the Nose, where it will take decades for new growth to get established.

"If the impact were happening today, we would stop it. But I think it's too late now," Shull explains. "We need to be realistic. We should turn our attention to protecting areas that still have a chance."

But getting that done may mean taking a more organized approach to monitoring climbing sites in the region. Limiting group size, providing "leave no trace" training, and delivering more restoration and site-management projects are a few starting points.

Brevard climbing guide Adam Fox has been a champion of the low-impact movement. "You can't point your finger at any one person," he says. "It's going to take everyone with a stake in the area to figure out how to avoid the overuse."

Still, the most persuasive enforcement may be the social sanctions imposed by fellow climbers. Longenecker recently approached a group at the base of the Nose and noticed several fresh branches of laurel and rhododendron lying in the sand. "I gave them their due," he recalls.

Despite the woeful condition at the base, 42 years later Longenecker still has proud memories of that cold, December day. He still has the threesome's original equipment, as well as news clippings about the Nose and Looking Glass Rock and snapshots of early climbs. Missing from his scrapbook, however, is an original photo of the base, unmarred by four decades of traffic. Hopefully, he'll find it some day.

Did *Bull Durham* Save the Minor Leagues?

"You play this game with fear and arrogance."

"Until you win 20 in the bigs, it just means you're a slob."

"Never punch out a drunk with your pitching hand."

"Don't think, meat. You'll only hurt the team."

If ever a movie came close to answering all life's questions, it was *Bull Durham*.

Released in 1988, and filmed almost entirely on location in North Carolina, *Bull Durham* was an affectionate and authentic look at life in minor league baseball. Writer and director Ron Shelton based the movie on his own experiences as a minor-leaguer. The plot, such as it was, centered around one season of the Durham Bulls, and the love triangle between baseball groupie Annie Savoy, hotshot rookie pitcher Ebby Calvin "Nuke" LaLoosh, and veteran catcher Crash Davis, brought in to show Nuke the ropes.

Though the cast included Susan Sarandon, Tim Robbins, and Kevin Costner, the old Durham Athletic Park was as much a star of the movie as any of the actors. Whatever designs Annie may have had on Nuke and Crash, the object of the truest love in the film was baseball itself. It's the love of the game that gets the players through the interminable bus rides through the Carolina piedmont, that keeps the managers "selling Lady Kenmores at Sears" to pay the bills while they await the next Opening Day, that brings the fans to run-down ballparks season after season. Durham Athletic Park was filmed as lovingly, was made as much an object of desire, as Sarandon.

The movie was a hit and an instant sports-movie classic. A 2003 issue of *Sports Illustrated* named it the greatest sports movie of all time.

But did *Bull Durham* save minor-league baseball?

No, probably not. Minor league baseball was in no danger of extinction in the late 1980s, but it was in decline. After *Bull Durham*'s release, though, minor league teams experienced a resurgence in attendance and merchandising sales. The movie's embrace of the . . . well, the *minor-league* aspects of the minor leagues seemed to remind baseball fans of what they loved about their local teams: the cheesy promotions ("Hit the Bull, Win a Steak"), the youthful hope of the players, the comfort of a stiff bleacher seat in an old ballpark.

The irony is that the success spurred by *Bull Durham* set off a process that saw much of the minor-league charm leached from the minor leagues. To cash in on the merchandising boom, farm teams began changing names every few years to groaningly odd monikers like "Warthogs" and "Crawdads." Ballparks were renovated, if not replaced, and calliopes gave way to pumped-up, piped-in pop music. Some minor league parks even added luxury boxes.

Only seven years after *Bull Durham*'s release, the Durham Bulls themselves replaced Durham Athletic Park with the $16 million Durham Bulls Athletic Park, designed by the same architects behind Camden Yards and Coors Field. The new field seats—and usually draws—10,000 spectators.

Rumors of a *Bull Durham* sequel have been around for a few years now, but they could no longer film it in the park that gave the original its soul. That soul was a big part of what made the movie a success, and that success is a big part of what killed off the soul.

—Ed Southern

A Triumph for Title IX

By Susan Shackleford

Sunday at the Richmond Coliseum, as I watched North Carolina win its first national title in women's basketball, an old movie played in my head.

It was 20 years ago. Watergate was still a minor burglary, gasoline was hard to come by and most people knew Ronald Reagan mainly as an actor. I was a sophomore at UNC-Chapel Hill and a sportswriter for the campus newspaper. After class one day, the women's basketball coach, Dr. Raye Holt, handed me a draft of a federal bill she said was soon to be passed by Congress. She replied, in Nike-esque foreshadowing, "Just read it."

I made my way through the lengthy draft of a document called "Title IX."

I called the coach and said, "This sounds like it will revolutionize college sports for women."

She said simply, "Yes."

I called all over the state asking college and other education administrators what Title IX was going to mean to their schools. They weren't aware of it. When I wrote about Title IX—which says colleges must offer equitable athletic treatment to women or risk losing their federal funding—it was picked up by the wire services. It was big news.

So why the old movie? I realized that because of Title IX women playing on this North Carolina team didn't grow up as women of my generation did: fighting mostly all-male administrations to keep what few athletic morsels were tossed our way.

When I first arrived at Carolina in 1972, the women played basketball in a cracker-box gym and no one was on scholarship. Today, scholarships are the norm and the team plays in Carmichael Auditorium, a 10,000-seat facility where the men played before the Dean Dome.

Title IX has not been a panacea. Violations of the law were largely ignored in the '80s and many coaches of women's teams are still woefully underpaid compared to their male counterparts. But it did lay the groundwork for generations of young women who know they don't have to check their competitive sports dreams at the college door.

They can dream of winning a scholarship, and of hitting a buzzer-beater to win the national championship—as Charlotte Smith of Shelby no doubt had done before she lofted her three-pointer with .7 seconds left in North Carolina's 60–59 victory Sunday.

Smith was asked if she wore No. 23 because of another famous Tar Heel who hit a jump shot to give

Originally published in the *Charlotte Observer*, April 5, 1994.

the North Carolina men's team a 1982 NCAA championship: Michael Jordan.

"I wasn't aware of that," Smith said. "I wear the number because it's the same one my mother wore in high school."

How fitting.

March 2008

By Michael Kruse

March 30, 2008.
Detroit.
Kansas 59, Davidson 57, and the clocks at Ford Field showed 16.8 seconds left.
Timeout.
Davidson ball.

Davidson College was one made shot from beating Kansas. One made shot from one of the most stunning upsets in the history of the sport. One made shot from the Final Four. To get to this moment, the Wildcats had gone undefeated in the Southern Conference, and then in the NCAA tournament they had beaten Gonzaga in the first round, and Georgetown in the second round, and Wisconsin in the third round.

Now this.

Now this moment.

It's a college that has an enrollment of only 1,700 students, and is in a small town, in the suburbs north of Charlotte, with a population of not even 10,000 people. It's a college that's hard to get into—only a quarter of the applicants do—and in 2008 it was ranked one of the top 10 colleges in the nation by *U.S. News & World Report*. It's a college that typically produces doctors and lawyers, preachers and Rhodes Scholars, not basketball stars.

"Davidson!" the CBS play-by-play man yelled now. "With life!"

America, one sports columnist wrote, had fallen "stone-cold in love." Davidson was the No. 1 search on Google after the Georgetown win. Davidson was mentioned 9,000 times in the print media in the month of March. Davidson.edu got 1.2 million hits. The Kansas game was watched by a record crowd of more than 57,000 at Ford Field in Detroit. Almost 14 million people watched it on CBS. Almost one in five televisions in the country that were turned on were turned on to see Davidson play Kansas.

There was Bob McKillop. He was the coach who had come to Davidson two decades before to try to get somewhere else, to go somewhere bigger, to earn a more lucrative contract. But the New Yorker had found his place in this tiny town in the South. Now, in news conferences, he talked eloquently about balance, and about discipline, and about loss, and about love.

There was Stephen Curry. He was the slim, slight guard who wasn't recruited by any of the many big schools in the area around his home in Charlotte but had turned into a high-scoring All-American. He was a sophomore, a superstar, with the first name with the funky pronunciation—STEFF-in—the just-turned 20-year-old who looked like a kid and shot like a pro and wrote Scripture on his sneakers. Two years at Davidson, and he had become the most important player in the college's basketball history; 10 days in the tournament, and he had become the nation's newest basketball darling.

There was Jason Richards. He was the gutsy, smiling, steady senior point guard. He had barely even played in his first two years on the team. As a junior, though, nobody in the conference had more assists than he did. And as a senior? Nobody in the country.

And there was the rest of the team, this interesting, international collection of selfless, well-drilled, hard-working kids from places like Cincinnati and Maine, France and Nigeria, Staten Island and Quebec. They were history majors, political science majors, economics majors and math majors, kids who were mostly unwanted and unknown coming out of high school, kids who were unheralded but not untalented, kids who had gotten better, and better, and better . . .

Sports columnists called the team "young America at its finest" and "a little slice of what's right." One even wrote before the game against Kansas that "a Davidson victory is what's best for the world."

The moment, the 16.8 seconds, at the end of the Kansas game—it was a moment watched by so many, but it also was a moment that had been created, by so many people for so many years doing so many things that were watched by so very few.

Until now.

Some people called it a Cinderella tale.

Some people called it a miracle.

But that wasn't true.

That wasn't what it was.

At least that's not all it was.

The story of Davidson's NCAA tournament run in 2008 was a story of second-half comebacks, and pictures on the front pages of newspapers of fresh faces of sheer joy; spray-painted GO CATS bed-sheet signs hung on porches by fans rooting for kids they actually knew, and alums who stood in the stands with tears in their eyes; and a whole sporting nation that looked at Davidson and saw in the team and the story something it wanted or needed to see.

☆ ☆ ☆

The camera shifted to the Davidson sideline.

McKillop, with his trim dark suit, his silver-white hair and his sharp blue eyes, looked at his team.

He was 57 years old and had won more games than any coach in school or conference history. He had been the league's coach of the year a record seven times. All 62 of his seniors had graduated. Before the '08 tournament, though, his team had never beaten a team ranked in the top 25. His team had never won a game in the NCAAs. So he had remained mostly anonymous to most fans of the sport. Within his profession, though, he was respected as a meticulous, almost professorial tactician, intense and ultra-competitive and yet finger-snap quick to tear up when talking about his family, or his team, or both.

He had many messages for the kids on his team.

One of them: Don't guard yourself. Don't let missteps in the past lead to more in the future.

Next play.

McKillop's career at Davidson had started 19 years

before, in old, hot Johnston Gym, in a small office with a window unit air conditioner and a red shag carpet. Davidson was decades past its basketball prime.

In 1960, folksy, strong-willed Lefty Driesell, so young at the time, came to coach the team at Davidson, which back then had mandated attendance at church services and an enrollment of less than 1,000 students, all men, in an area that was all red dirt and rural. Basketball success was unlikely. But Driesell's first team beat Wake Forest in its first game, and he started recruiting players who went on to become All-Americans, and by the time he left to coach at Maryland, in 1969, he had taken Davidson to four finishes in the nation's top 10 and consecutive trips to the regional finals.

The decade of Driesell made basketball the flagship sport at the college.

It set a precedent.

Driesell had been a high school coach in Virginia before coming to Davidson. McKillop was not so different on that point. He had been a high school coach in New York, at Trinity High in Hicksville, at Long Island Lutheran in Brooksville, and had gone to eight state Final Fours in 13 years. And when he arrived at Davidson, in 1989, he put in his office a copy of the *Sports Illustrated* from 1964 in which Davidson was ranked No. 1 in the country.

McKillop said he was going to do that again.

That first summer, when he had moved down to Davidson and his family was still up on Long Island, he called one of the players on his new team.

He asked if he was a dreamer.

"Understand," the coach said. "I'm expecting big things."

He told his new team in the first team meeting in the fall of '89 that *he* was on a mission and that *they* were invited to come along. Then he made them do wind sprints on the track and five-mile runs around campus in the semi-dark of hazy early mornings. Hurricane Hugo came through the Carolinas in September and knocked a big tree down across the track. He told them to run around it. He called them fat and slow in the locker room after a loss on the road. He didn't turn the heat on in the bus back to the airport. At one point he tied an electrical socket to his torso and implored his players to "plug into him" if they needed energy. It didn't work. His players wanted to believe in him. They did not.

McKillop had done nothing but win in high school. He thought he was going to do nothing but win in college.

His first year at Davidson ended with a record of four wins and 24 losses.

His second year: 10 and 19.

The third: 11 and 17.

The breaking point came at the end of that season. In Anderson, South Carolina, Davidson lost in the conference tournament quarter-finals. This was early March of 1992. The Davidson booster club had rented a room at the Holiday Inn. Cold cuts. Post-game bottles of Bud. Maybe 15 people showed up. McKillop gave a short talk. People who were there said it felt like a wake. It was raining outside, hard, and McKillop left, he left his wife and his three young children, and he left the hotel to go watch a recruit who was playing nearby. He drove away, through the rain, straining to see what was ahead.

He questioned himself. He questioned his decision to leave New York, where he grew up, where he had started a family and a life, where he had been comfortable. He doubted his ability to win at Davidson, ever, or in college at all. He had come to Davidson to win, and to win fast, so he could move on to a more prestigious job. It was about him, and what he was going to do, and how he was going to do it—and it wasn't working.

He had to think about that, about why it wasn't working.

That electrical socket gimmick?

Energy, he realized, isn't a one-way deal. Everyone has energy. The point is to share it.

"I came to the conclusion," he would say years later, "that I had done a disservice to my players by thinking only what winning would do for me.... I decided to tell the guys that winning and losing doesn't matter. But if we care about each other, and show we care about each other, winning will take care of itself."

He decided on a three-word code for the basketball program at Davidson.

Trust. Commitment. Care.

Those three words started as letters printed on T-shirts and painted on locker-room signs. Slowly, though, they started to mean more than that.

McKillop stayed just as intense but without such a hard edge. His players started to notice a change. Cockiness became confidence. The McKillop who used to jab an elbow into players' chests to test toughness and jam knives into tables in hotel ballrooms to teach killer instinct now almost never let one of his players come off the court without a touch of the hand. More and more, one player said, he was "hand-across-your-back" McKillop. The older he gets, the more he learns, McKillop told one of his assistant coaches, the more he cries.

McKillop could have left Davidson in 1994. But he had just been to his first conference championship game with Davidson. He came close to leaving in '98. But he had just been to his first NCAA tournament with Davidson. He came close again in '99. But his daughter had just finished her freshman year at Davidson. She ended up marrying a Davidson man in a Davidson church. McKillop's older son went to Davidson and played for the team. His younger son followed. McKillop lives across the street from campus. He walks to the gym for games. He has called the little village Camelot. It's the McKillop parable: He came to Davidson to go somewhere else, and ended up finding a home. It became his home because it became his family's home.

And over the years he honed the system that came to define the Davidson basketball program. It was a system that fit the college and the place, and he started recruiting kids who could work, and work well, within both.

McKillop grew up a skinny-necked altar boy in Queens, in a small row house with a low concrete stoop, and he was the fourth-shortest boy in his First Communion class. He was cut from his freshman basketball team, and from his junior varsity team, and from his varsity team as a junior. He made the varsity team only as a senior. He started only one game in high school, and yet he played college ball at East Carolina and then Hofstra, and improved enough to earn an NBA tryout.

For Davidson, some believe, he recruits players who remind him of *him*: too small, too slow, overlooked.

McKillop and his assistant coaches look for qualities in prospects that go beyond running and jumping and shooting.

What does a kid do when his coach takes him out of the game? Does he walk over to the bench or does he run? How does he sit? Does he mope? Does he cheer for his teammates out on the floor? Does he high-five them?

Does he take big shots? Does he want to?

Loose ball on the floor. Does he dive head-first or is he scared?

Is he an eye-roller?

Is he a shoulder-shrugger?

Does he know the janitor with the keys to the gym?

How does he talk to his mother?

McKillop used to give a lecture at the summer camps he ran when he was a high-school coach. One time he called a boy out of the bleachers and gave him a thin, wood paint-stirring stick.

"Break it," he told the boy.

The boy broke it.

He gave the boy two of the sticks stacked together.

"Break them."

The boy broke them.

Then he gave the boy five of the sticks stacked together.

"Break them."

The boy could not.

One five, McKillop believed, and preached, even back then, is harder to break than five ones.

These lessons are passed from class to class at Davidson, little things that aren't little things. On offense: sharp passes, precise cuts, stout screens. On defense: no easy dribbles, no easy passes, all-out effort all the time. They practice tiny actions that happen over and over in games. Tapping out offensive rebounds. Saving loose balls near the sideline. Even running over to McKillop for timeouts. They develop habits. A bed, a former player once said, doesn't get made military-style just once. "Attack the attacker," McKillop tells his kids.

When we win, Davidson wins, he tells them. Nothing alone, he tells them. Everything together.

Now, inside this moment, inside Ford Field in Detroit, McKillop had been at Davidson for 19 years.

There are in the system seven keys of Davidson basketball.

The first key is to have an act.

The second is to see.

The third is to talk.

The fourth is to have no fear of flesh-to-flesh contact.

The fifth is balance.

The sixth is details.

And the seventh?

The seventh key is to *finish*.

☆ ☆ ☆

McKillop looked at his players now in the huddle on the sideline. He asked if they wanted to run the play they call Flat. The play is called Flat because the first important action in the play is a flat ball screen. That's when a post player comes from under the basket to the top of the key and sets a screen with his back parallel to the baseline. A teammate dribbles toward the screen and goes either right or left. The aim is to free the man with the ball by screening his defender. Davidson in 2008 ran Flat for pretty much just one guy. McKillop looked at Stephen now.

The boy-faced son of former NBA star Dell Curry had become a star himself. His season had been one of the nation's best—almost 26 points per game, Southern Conference player of the year, Associated Press All-American—and now he was not only the best player of the tournament but the best story.

The kid who looked like the kid next door, or the kid who cut your grass, or the water boy, scored 40 points against Gonzaga, 30 of them in the second half, and the Gonzaga coach told reporters his players probably had guarded him as well as they could. He scored 30 points against Georgetown, 25 of them in the second half, and the Georgetown coach said his defenders had been "all over him." He scored 33 points against Wisconsin in a 17-point win to get to the game against Kansas.

All this after he had picked Davidson over other small schools like Virginia Commonwealth and Winthrop. The big basketball programs at Atlantic Coast Conference and Southeastern Conference schools didn't want him. The only ACC school that recruited him even a little was Virginia Tech, and that was his parents' alma mater, and even there the coaches wanted him to walk on his first year. He was just so small. He was 5-feet-6 as a freshman at Charlotte Christian, so thin the coaches put him on the junior varsity team, and still only 5-feet-8 as a sophomore, and 5-feet-11 as a junior. He hit 6 feet only in his senior year. A typical scouting evaluation started like this: "Way overmatched from a physical standpoint."

But McKillop watched Stephen in layup lines when he was in high school. He wasn't "cool." Cool, the coach thought, is someone who wants people to watch. A sense of entitlement. There was none of that, he thought, with Stephen. Something else he noticed, and his assistants, too, was that Stephen's face almost never changed, no matter what. Made shot? Missed shot? Great pass? Bad pass? His face didn't change. His demeanor was calm. He didn't panic. He looked young. He looked little. But he looked like he was in control.

Meanwhile, his father was in the stands, helping to hang signs on the walls of the gym, and his mother was in the stands, keeping the scorebook. McKillop saw the kid came from a family that was strong and a family that was there.

And he saw improvement.

Stephen kept getting better.

In the spring of 2006, Davidson graduated seven seniors from a team that made the NCAA tournament, and fans were worried. Who was left? McKillop didn't seem too concerned.

Stephen showed up at Davidson for freshman orientation in August of 2006 with a microwave, his laptop, four duffel bags and a quilt he got from his grandmother as a high-school graduation gift. He was bigger, stronger, faster. Better. But that's not what struck the Davidson coaches the most. Stephen was able to take the information given to him in workouts and practices and correct his mistakes almost immediately. McKillop, even with three-and-a-half decades of coaching basketball, had never seen anything like it. It was as if, he thought, Stephen listened to what he was told, painted a picture of the movements in his head, and then funneled those movements onto the court, at full speed, the very next play.

It wasn't like Stephen never made mistakes.

He made a lot of mistakes.

He just didn't make too many mistakes twice.

In the first game of his college career, against Eastern Michigan, he had 13 turnovers.

In his second game, against Michigan in Ann Arbor, he had 32 points.

The Stephen Curry story took off from there: league freshman of the year, league tournament most valuable player, a college record for three-pointers in a season by a rookie, 30 points against Maryland in the NCAA tournament. Then, as a sophomore, more, more, more: 37 against Chattanooga, 38 against Appalachian, 41 against UNC-Greensboro. League player of the year, league tournament MVP again, All-American, a college record for three-pointers in a season, not by a rookie now, but by anybody ever. Along the way, middle-aged men, Davidson men, serious men with serious jobs, started showing up to games at Davidson wearing red No. 30 jerseys.

Now in Detroit the referees blew their whistles. The huddle broke and Stephen got up and started to walk up the sideline. Written in neat black Sharpie print on the side of his left red-and-white Nike was "I can do all things . . ." Philippians 4:13. "I can do all things through Christ who gives me strength." He made a fist with his right hand and hit his chest by his heart and then pointed with his finger up high. Stephen pointed a lot when he was out on the court. Throughout the season he had pointed a lot, to his teammates when they passed him the ball, to fans in the stands. Against Gonzaga, in the tournament, he had made a critical three-pointer and pointed to his father in the front row, the way Dell Curry used to point to his father, many years ago. That's Stephen: he takes the praise and tries to turn it around. He tries to widen the spotlight.

His teammates felt that.

Junior post player Andrew Lovedale described the spotlight on Stephen as family wealth. If your brother is rich, he explained, you're rich, too.

☆ ☆ ☆

Jason Richards took the court, too.

The senior point guard from Barrington, Illinois, had gone from little-used his first two years at Davidson to the best point guard in school history. All Jason did was take the ball where he wanted to take it, where he needed to take it, against just about everybody, just about always. He didn't see his teammates when they were open. He saw them when they were *getting* open. Pause a Davidson game tape, as opposing coaches did, over and over, and there was the ball, in the air, between Jason's hand and a spot on the floor where Stephen was *about* to be.

Jason didn't run the team's plays. Jason ran the team.

For many, it was hard to fathom; such improvement from the start of his career to now. But there were signs along the way.

When Jason was a freshman in high school, back in the Chicago suburbs, the basketball coach put him on the varsity team when he was a freshman. He was 5-feet-6, Jason was, and all of 120 pounds—he was prepubescent—but he was so skilled, the coach thought, that he could play varsity. But was he ready mentally? The coach called Jason's father. Was it O.K.? Was it O.K. if Jason played on the varsity team? The father told the coach that Jason always had played against older kids, stronger kids, and against his older sister, too, who was a high-school All-American, and so Jason had learned to hide what he couldn't do and to take advantage of what he could.

He didn't only *play* on the varsity team his freshman year. He *started*. And he played through taunts from fans of opposing teams.

"Where's your mommy?" they hollered at him.

The first time any coach from Davidson saw Jason

play was about a year-and-a-half after that. It was at a club team tournament in Orlando and one of Jason's games went six overtimes. Club team basketball is about showcasing individual skills. It's not about who wins tournaments; it's *me*, not *we*. But Davidson assistant Jim Fox sat in the stands for that game and watched Jason, in a six-overtime game in the summer, and he could see that Jason wanted to win, and wanted to win badly.

Davidson started recruiting him.

The next summer he kept getting better. He was small but smart. He understood what he could do, but also, and maybe more importantly, what he could not. He wasn't the quickest kid on the court but he had a fast first step and he used it to get by his defender, even just a little, and once he did that, he knew how to use his shoulders and his hips to stay that single step ahead. On one day, in a tournament in Kentucky, he made game-winning buzzer-beaters in three different games. His teammates started putting the ball in his hands at the ends of games. He had what the coach of his team started to think of as some kind of intangible "edge," a belief that he could play against anybody—everybody—and that belief seemed to turn contagious with his teammates.

They began to believe they could beat anybody.

Early on in his Davidson career, though, people weren't so sure. McKillop is known for how hard he is on point guards in practice. He's particularly hard on freshmen, even harder on point guards who are freshmen, and the very hardest on point guards who are freshmen who in his mind have the greatest potential. He was relentless with Jason.

Jason played only eight minutes a game as a backup his freshman year. As a sophomore, he showed occasional promise, but that year in the NCAA tournament, against Ohio State, he played poorly. He played scared and he knew it. After the game, back at the team's hotel, Jason was with his father in the lobby, and McKillop came over to them.

"Twelve o'clock rule," the coach told Jason.

Jason had until midnight to think about it.

Then it was over.

Then it was back to getting better.

"There's no time to relax," McKillop once wrote to him in an e-mail. "There's no time to take a breather. There's no time to think you have it made.

"Nor," the coach wrote, "is there time to think you can't make it."

Jason had 13 assists and no turnovers in Davidson's win over Wisconsin. One of the Wisconsin players said he was the best point guard he had ever played against.

Now on the court at Ford Field, Jason ran down to the right corner and took his place for the game's final play.

Time started to tick off the clock: 16 . . .

. . . 15 . . .

. . . 14 . . .

☆ ☆ ☆

Up in the stands were Davidson alums ranging from the 1930s to incoming freshmen. The game had turned into the biggest, best-attended reunion ever, nearly a century in the life of the college. Almost all the trustees had contributed their own money to pay to bus nearly a third of the student body to Detroit. The Dearborn Doubletree had become a Davidson dorm. There, students had sat at tables in the lobby and spread out around the floor and opened their laptops and worked on papers and tests; here, inside Ford Field, they held signs high above their heads.

WHY NOT?

THOU SHALL NOT DOUBT

They were chanting.

"We believe!"

"We believe!"

Many of them were wearing new red shirts that had on the front one word written in a white block font. WITNESS. The shirts had been handed out by the school for the Wisconsin game, and they seemed appropriate that night because LeBron James, the NBA star who uses the word as one of his Nike marketing phrases, was in a seat a few rows behind the bench, there, he said, "to watch the kid." Stephen. The WITNESS shirts were cool, but not quite right, some of the students thought. They didn't feel like they were just watching this. They felt like they were a part of it. They knew all the guys down there on the court. Davidson was a small, small school, small campus, and they studied for calculus with them, they ate at the same cafeteria, they played pick-up basketball together on the outdoor courts.

What they shared, the students off the court, and the students on it, was a place: a college with white-pillar buildings and red-brick walkways, a town with one bar, a barbershop, a bookstore and a greasy spoon called the Soda Shop on a Main Street that looked like a painting by Norman Rockwell; and a campus where life was dictated by Davidson's Honor Code, which meant community bikes anyone could use, unsupervised exams, lost watches returned, lost dollar bills tacked to bulletin boards.

Now down on the court, Bryant Barr, a guard from Maine, ran to the left corner of the court. He was Stephen's roommate. The two of them went to church together Sunday mornings. He was a good shooter, too, and Stephen had told him in the huddle to be ready for the ball.

Steve Rossiter had passed the ball in to Stephen and now he ran to the left low block. He had the only visible tattoo on the team. It was on his right shoulder and said FEARLESS. Back in his senior year of high school in Staten Island, McKillop was there to watch him play and Rossiter had one of his worst games. In the second half, though, he was sitting on the bench and his backup scored and he stood up and cheered. McKillop offered him a scholarship after the game. Now he was considered the second-best screen setter on the team.

The best screen setter on the team—the best screen setter McKillop had ever had—was Thomas Sander. He was going to be the one to set the screen at the top of the key to trigger the play, Flat. Sander grew up in Cincinnati and went to Elder High, a Catholic, community service-oriented school on the city's hard-working west side, and his role on the team at Davidson was to do all types of things that didn't show up on a stat sheet. He anchored the defense. He took charges. He set screens. He played most of the tournament with a thumb he'd broken in the first half against Gonzaga. He got shots of painkillers in the thumb before the next three games. They made his thumb so numb he sometimes had to look down to make sure he had the ball in his hands. Still, though, he played. Every one of his teammates, he thought to himself, would have done the same thing for him.

Now he started to move toward the top of the key to set the screen for Stephen.

Up in the stands, a student, a sophomore, felt the way he had felt right before he proposed to his girlfriend over Christmas break. Everything had led to this moment. He had the ring. All he had to do was reach down and pull it out of his pocket. All he had to do was ask.

Two words kept running through his head.

Say yes.

Say yes.

Say yes.

Down closer to the court an alum, Class of '02, felt the way she had felt after the bridesmaids had gone away, when it was just her and her father, and the music changed, and the wedding director opened the doors, and all that was left was to be surrounded by people she loved and to walk from the vestibule into the sanctuary, and down the aisle, and up to the altar.

Now she watched Stephen dribble the ball up the court.

In Washington, D.C., another alum, Class of '95, sat alone in front of his DVR-equipped TV, and he realized he wasn't ready for any of this. He wasn't ready for a shot to miss, and he wasn't even ready for a shot to be made, because what happens when a dream stops being a dream and all of a sudden turns real?

So he picked up his remote.

And he hit pause.

He thought about the previous 10 days.

He thought about all the stories in the news all over the country about his alma mater. "The face of this NCAA tournament." "The Wizard of Oz in short pants." "A message for the world."

He thought about the text message he had gotten that week from another alum.

"It's like a dream," it had said.

But now he looked at his cell phone.

It hadn't buzzed.

It was still, it was silent, and he knew. He unpaused his television. Not to see what had happened but to see how.

Stephen had crossed halfcourt.

Nine seconds left.

Thomas set the screen. Stephen's defender fell to the floor. Stephen darted left.

Seven seconds.

Jason was still in the right corner. He watched Stephen stop going to his left and turn back to his right and start heading toward another screen set by Thomas.

Six seconds.

Jason watched another Kansas defender duck past Thomas and chase Stephen. He watched Stephen's defender get back up off the floor and start chasing Stephen, too.

Five seconds.

Jason decided he had to move. He didn't want this game to end with him just standing in the corner. He didn't want to be watching.

He wanted to help.

So he started running toward Stephen.

Four seconds.

Stephen pump-faked. His defender jumped up and off to the side. Maybe here was a sliver of an opening for a shot. But Jason's defender left Jason now and bolted toward Stephen. His arms were straight up.

The opening closed.

Three seconds.

Stephen had only one option.

Jason was maybe 25 feet from the basket. He was

to the right of the center of the court. He let the ball go with 1.3 seconds left. A camera flash. Another. More. Then the red light and the buzzer. Jason put both hands up to cover his face. He hit the floor, first with his butt, then with his back. Bryant Barr was the first to get to him. Steve Rossiter was next. Then Thomas Sander. Don't let a teammate stay down on the floor: part of trust, commitment, care. They helped him up. Jason leaned over. He put his hands on his knees. He untucked his shirt. He started to walk off the court. He walked down a tunnel and back toward the locker room. He heard the crowd.

"Great run!"

"Head up!"

☆ ☆ ☆

In Davidson, in the college union, there were thousands of people packed into the rooms, and first there had been silence.

But then there was clapping.

And then there was more.

In Detroit the locker room was silent. Stephen sat at the end of a row of chairs and stared at the floor. Jason sat to his left and had his head in his hands. McKillop put his right hand on the top of Jason's head and he held it there.

The team went back to the hotel before the flight home. Lindsay Richards was in the lobby waiting to see her brother.

"He came in on the bus," she said later. "We were already there. Jason has always been a fighter. . . . He's pretty good at bouncing back from things. But because this was such a bigger scale you just don't know. So he came in. And everyone was clapping. And he walked straight to my dad. Rarely do my dad and my brother cry. My dad held his head on his shoulder. And when Jason pulled away, his eyes were watering, and my dad's were, too. I didn't go to him for a while. I just watched. I didn't want to be crying when I went to him. I wanted to be stronger. I didn't want to be the sister who was tugging on him. So he came over to me. I was on the other side of the room. He came to me, and he gave me a hug, a bear hug, and he said: 'Are you crying?' I said no. He said: 'Why are you crying?' He said: 'Come on. Stop it. Stop crying.

'There's still more.'

"That's what he said.

'There's still more.'"

☆ ☆ ☆

Two days later, William Robertson, Davidson Class of '75 and the chaplain at the North Carolina state mental hospital in Morganton, sat in his small office in the chapel where he worked and he started to write.

"I've seen some pictures of Stephen Curry since Sunday, and he has been smiling," he wrote. "I haven't seen any pictures of Jason, but I hope he's smiling also. Because the last play of that great game was a very good play. It was probably the perfect play."

He posted what he wrote on the message board at DavidsonCats.com.

He said that McKillop trusted his players, and that Stephen trusted Jason by passing him the ball, and that Jason trusted that he still would be loved even if he missed that shot.

He quoted Teddy Roosevelt.

". . . those cold and timid souls who know neither victory nor defeat . . ."

He quoted Faulkner in *Intruder in the Dust*.

"... all this much to lose and all this much to gain ..."

He quoted Shakespeare in *Henry V*.

"This story shall the good man teach his son."

He thought about Davidson's moment.

"In that moment," Robertson wrote, "we had in our hearts and minds, proleptically I think the theologians would say, the joy of having it go in. Before it was not in, it was as good as in. For that fraction of a second, we had that experience, and it is enough. It is well worth the journey. At least for me it is, and I guess the ultimate point of this too-long post is that I hope it is also worth it for Jason. He took the shot. He gave us that moment. He trusted, and all we can do is be sure our reaction is worthy of that trust."

A Tuesday evening in April.

McKillop stood on a stage set up on the court at Belk Arena in Davidson in front of thousands of fans still wanting all of it not to be over. He stood in front of his players seated in chairs on the stage and he turned to talk to them.

"The arena's going to empty out," the coach said. "The lights are going to be turned off. You're going to go back to your rooms. And in the silence of your rooms you're going to think about this particular night and think about this season and then you're going to wake up and understand that you lived this season with a dedication to commit yourselves to excellence. You lived this season with a dedication to commit yourselves to care for each other as teammates and you lived this season trusting each other, trusting yourselves, trusting your coaches—in good times and in bad—to do the right thing.

"Headlines are going to fade. Trophies? They're going to tarnish. But the relationships you have built this year, built upon trust, care and commitment, will last for your lifetimes."

He turned back around and faced the crowd.

"You can go to any library in America," he said. "You can go to any bookstore, and find row after row and shelf after shelf of self-help books. How to get better. How to live your life correctly. I've read many. But I come back always to one of the great books of all time.

"The Bible. Micah. Chapter 6."

He paused.

"Act justly," he said.

"Love tenderly."

"Walk humbly with your God."

The thousands of people broke the silence and clapped and clapped and then they stopped and it was silent again.

"That's the challenge that we now face," McKillop told the people. "We are an elite team. We are on a pedestal. We are on the Broadway stage.

"We need your prayers. We need your support. We need your help. We need your guidance.

"We need you," he said, "to hold us accountable as we continue to chase our dreams."

A Thursday evening in May.

Jason Richards stood behind a podium in front of hundreds of fans sitting at tables arranged under a huge tent outside at the team's annual year-end banquet. He gave his senior speech. He talked about his four years at Davidson and on the team, and he started to cry.

"Sorry," he said.

Silence.

Finally, from near the rear of the tent, a voice.

"Don't be sorry."

Weeks passed.

Months passed.

People around Davidson still were talking about the 10 days of the tournament and the moment in Detroit. They talked about hope and possibility and things larger than self. They said things like this: "It turned everybody into children." And this: "We found something we didn't know we had lost." And this: "We're all seeking it. We're all wanting it. And there it was." And this: "Everybody dies. The point is to live a full and beautiful life. But everybody dies." And they were asking questions: What was it? What was I watching? And what *is* winning?

People cried, months later, just thinking about it.

Strange, though, many of them said. They cared about that moment, in the moment and since, and deeply. They just didn't so much care if the ball actually went in. They were not so much upset by how it ended. They were upset that it had to end at all.

☆ ☆ ☆

The moment ended.

The moment kept going.

Davidson College finished the 2008 academic year ranked ninth in the *U.S. News & World Report* academic rankings, and ninth, too, in the *USA Today* basketball poll.

Over the summer many of the guys on the team got TCC tattoos. TRUST. COMMITMENT. CARE. The code of Davidson basketball had started as printed words on T-shirts. It had started as painted words on signs on walls. Now it was ink on skin forever.

Jason signed a contract with the Miami Heat of the NBA and played with the team before hurting his knee.

Thomas decided not to play professionally and started working for a bank in New York. He said he didn't miss playing basketball. He just missed playing basketball for Davidson.

Stephen came back. In November he scored 44 points against Oklahoma. In December he scored 44 points against N.C. State. Three days after that, up in New York, in front of a raucous crowd at Madison Square Garden that was there mostly to see him, he hit two late three-pointers to beat West Virginia, and West Virginia coach Bob Huggins said: "I don't think we've seen anything like him in college basketball for decades."

He scored the 2,000th point of his college career before the start of the second semester of his junior year. Former Indiana coach Bob Knight said on ESPN that Stephen was "as good a passer as has ever played college basketball."

In January tickets for Davidson's game at Duke were selling on the Internet for $1,200.

Davidson's games at home were sold out.

Davidson's games on the road were sold out.

"We are blessed," one fan wrote on DavidsonCats.com. He wrote that this, all this, was not just about one player, but about "a basketball team that we dreamed of when we were children. One that we never truly thought we'd see at Davidson. . . .

"We get," he said, "to watch the electricity crackle."

Before one game in Davidson, in early January, people were outside Belk Arena, in the cold, holding signs saying they needed tickets. There was an older man. There was a father with his toddler daughter.

They were holding up two fingers, both of them, looking for a way in.

This for a Southern Conference game. On January 3. Over Christmas break. With no students on campus.

Athletic department staffers who have been at Davidson for any length of time remember game days, in the '90s, walking around town trying to give people tickets. Here. Just take them. No cost. Just please come.

Sometimes these days those staffers stand at games and have full hearts and wet eyes as they look around, at 5,223 in Belk, crammed in, every game, all the time, all the way up to the roof, making all that noise for their boys dressed in white and red.

Everything is different.

Nothing is different.

The goal was never to make the regional finals. The goal was never to make the Final Four. The goal was to play so hard, and so well, and so together—so much like a team—that such a thing even could become a possibility.

People saw something.

They saw something they wanted to see.

And they couldn't stop watching.

The story didn't end.

The story kept going.

2
THE TEAMS

The Incredible True Story of the 1951 Rocks

By Matthew Musson

Back in 1951, before watching television became the national pastime, baseball history was made in the Blue Ridge Mountains of North Carolina. That spring the town of Granite Falls, just north of Hickory, replaced the failed Gastonia Browns franchise in the celebrated Western Carolina League. And, in that 1951 season, the Granite Falls Graniteers achieved a milestone that has never been equaled: They chalked up the worst record in the history of professional baseball in America.

On April 13th, 1951, veteran Boston Red Sox pitcher Charlie Bowles signed on to skipper the Graniteers. And, just ten days later, Granite Falls took the field for the very first time, squaring off against a New York Giants farm team, the Lenoir Red Sox.

As Wilt Browning describes in his book *The Rocks*, Granite Falls—the 1948, 1949 and 1950 Carolina Mill League champions—quickly learned the difference between amateur and professional baseball. The Graniteers were hammered 13–3 in their initial outing. Six more painful lessons followed, before they hit the longest winning streak of the '51 season: back to back wins against Marion and Lenoir.

The Graniteers went through five coaches in their 14 and 96 struggle. They finished 57 games out of first place and an astounding 26 games out of seventh, in an eight-team league. The Graniteers failed to win a single game in August and were winless in their last 32 outings.

Even "Black Cat Night" (all fans carrying a live black cat got in free) and changing the team's name to the Granite Rocks did not improve their fortune. Before the season ended, one coach actually traded himself away, and the official scorekeeper quit coming to the stadium.

Granite Falls dropped 57 of their last 58 games. With their winning percentage of 0.1272, they displaced the 1899 Cleveland Spiders as the worst team in baseball.

But the '51 Rocks were not done making history.

In late August, with the Rocks 23 games out of seventh place, owner Finley German exercised the freedom of having nothing left to lose. In a home doubleheader against the Cleveland Indians-affiliated Newton-Conover Twins, three African-American players debuted for Granite Falls.

This was two years before second baseman Henry Aaron reported to the Jacksonville team of the Class AA Southern League. It was 1951, in North Carolina, and African Americans were not served in "white" restaurants, they drank from "colored" drinking fountains, and they still rode in the back of the bus.

But in Granite Falls, the times were changing.

Because the Rocks' scorekeeper abandoned the team, it is not surprising there are no official box scores for the first integrated baseball game in North Carolina history. But what is startling is the news outlets of the day almost completely ignored the milestone. In fact, the only published report of the game appeared three days later in the Monday Baseball Summary of the *Hickory Daily Record*. Buried in the fourth and fifth paragraphs it was noted:

> "The first Negro players to see action in the Class D Western Carolina League played for Granite Falls. All three of the colored men to play hail from Ridgeview at Hickory. Russell Shuford worked behind the plate the major portion of both games for the Rocks. Christopher Rankin pitched two innings of the first game and two-and-two-thirds innings in the second game. Gene Abernathy, one of Ridgeview's top all-around athletes, went in as a pinch-hitter in the first game and played center field in the second game. Neither of the trio got a hit and Shuford was charged with two errors."

The second game marked Granite Falls' 27th straight loss, breaking their earlier record of 26 straight.

On the following Wednesday, August 29, the Rocks dropped their next game to Marion. The *Daily Record* mentioned this loss in their Western Carolina Baseball Roundup:

> "With four Negro's in the lineup—the first to play on a white baseball team in North Carolina—the Granite Falls Rocks went down in favor of Marion's Marauders, 10–3. The negroes were Bill Smith of Newton, a catcher; Boney Flemming of Asheville, formerly a pitcher for the Negro Asheville Blues; Christopher Rankin of Hickory, a right-handed pitcher; and Gene Abernathy of Hickory, an outfielder. Another negro, Russell Shuford, a catcher, is also with the club, but not in action after suffering a broken finger."

The Rocks followed up by dropping a double header at Lincolnton, for which only the final scores are known: 5–4 and 8–1.

Finally, on September 1st, 1951, the Granite Falls Rocks played their 110th and final game, on the road, against the league-leading Morganton Aggies. The Rocks were on a 31-game losing streak, but they were not giving up. They scored two runs in the eighth and tied the game. The next inning was scoreless and at the end of nine it was a 4–4 standoff.

With strong pitching from former Negro Leaguer Boney Flemming, four scoreless innings followed. Granite Falls battled toe-to-toe with the league champions, and for one brief shining moment, it seemed possible that the Rocks might earn that 15th win and move ahead of Cleveland in the record books. Unfortunately, as the *Record* reported, "Hal Harris walked to start the Morganton fourteenth, moved to second on a wild pitch, reached third on Buck McAnulty's single, and scooted home on Fred Parnell's one-base poke."

Granite Falls lost their final contest, 5–4, in 14 innings. The Rocks' one and only season ended, and Finley German and the five brave young men who integrated Carolina baseball were all but forgotten. To this very day there is still no marker at Granite Falls's Howard Deal Baseball Stadium, where the 1951 Graniteers/Rocks made baseball history—twice.

The Cardiac Pack

You didn't have to be a fan. If you were living in the Carolinas in April 1983, you probably remember where you were when the Cardiac Pack won. If you were watching, you jumped out of your chair. If you weren't, you heard the hollering from living rooms, bars, dorm lounges, and wherever else people were gathered.

North Carolina State University was the greatest underdog since Jesus took on sin. The Houston Cougars had won 26 straight. They were rich in talent and nicknames, most of them coined by Houston graduate Jim Nantz, a local announcer at the time. "Phi Slama Jama." Clyde "the Glide" Drexler, first-team All-American and future NBA Hall of Famer. Akeem "the Dream" Olajuwon, also a future Hall of Famer and for a couple of years the best player in the world. Larry "Mr. Mean" Micheaux. Michael "Silent Assassin" Young.

And the opponent from Raleigh? Well, it had Lorenzo Charles, the redoubtable "Lorilla."

But make no mistake, N.C. State was no Wusspack. Seniors Sidney Lowe and Dereck Whittenburg were one of the most experienced and best-rounded guard tandems in the country, backed by sophomore Terry Gannon. Senior Thurl Bailey and sophomores Charles and Cozell McQueen were a big and capable trio inside. Bailey went on to a 14-year career in the NBA. Lowe played four years in the pros, while Charles and McQueen had short stays. McQueen actually finished his NBA career with a perfect 1.000 field goal percentage and shocking averages of 41 points and 55 rebounds factored over a 48-minute game. The punch line is that he played a total of seven minutes.

The Wolfpack got off to a 7–1 start, including victories over Michigan State, West Virginia, and Clemson. Following a loss to Missouri, N.C. State was up by double digits in the first half against Virginia, the number-two team in the country, when Whittenburg broke his foot. The Pack lost 88–80 and subsequently slid to 9–7 overall and 3–4 in the ACC. It regrouped to win eight of 11 the rest of the way, completing the regular season at 17–10. The finale, a whopping 130–89 victory over Wake Forest, avenged an 18-point loss to the Deacons earlier in the year.

Still, few people suspected something special was happening in Raleigh. The Pack's 8–6 ACC record tied it for third in the conference.

Some teams are defined by their players—like Houston by Drexler and Olajuwon and Virginia by towering Ralph Sampson. But N.C. State was defined by Jim Valvano, its coach. Valvano was born in New York City and played point guard at Rutgers, graduating in 1967 with a degree in English. He coached at Johns Hopkins, Bucknell, and Iona before being hired by N.C. State in 1980. Some coaches—like Dean Smith and Mike Krzyzewski—

assimilate so well that fans tend to forget they're from someplace else. But Valvano never seemed to try, always remaining an unabashed New Yorker. He was a funny guy, the kind who could grouse about the pizza in the Carolinas without offending anyone. He was part inspirational leader, part shyster.

The excitement started at the ACC Tournament in Atlanta, the Pack needing to win to make the national field. Standing in the way were Virginia and Michael Jordan's UNC Tar Heels. The good news? The return to form of Dereck Whittenburg, who had struggled since coming back from his injury.

N.C. State faced Wake Forest in the opening round. Their two regular-season games had been blowouts, one each way, but the third meeting was tight, the Wolfpack winning 71–70 behind Thurl Bailey's 25 points. In the semi-finals, Michael Jordan fouled out with 3:42 remaining and State up by five, but UNC rallied to send the game to overtime, where it took a commanding six-point lead. Then Whittenburg scored nine straight points during a 15–2 State run in the final two minutes to close out a frenetic 91–84 win. The finals saw the Wolfpack, a two-time loser to Virginia during the regular season, beat the Cavaliers 81–78.

The field was expanded from 48 to 52 teams for the 1983 national tournament. N.C. State was shipped out west to Oregon to face Pepperdine. The Wolfpack prevailed 69–67 in double overtime, Whittenburg scoring 22 and Lorenzo Charles grabbing 14 rebounds. In the next nail-biter, Thurl Bailey's 25 points led the Pack past UNLV, 71–70. By then, Valvano's simple directive to his players—he kept telling them to put themselves "in a position to win" late in games—was becoming a mantra.

State had its only easy game of the tournament when it beat Utah 75–56 in the West Regionals in Utah. Then came a fourth meeting with Virginia. The Wolfpack was down by one late when Whittenburg had an open jumper for the win. Instead, he passed to Charles under the basket, where he was fouled by Ralph Sampson with 23 seconds left. Charles made both free throws to end Sampson's college career. The three-time national player of the year never won an ACC or an NCAA championship.

The Pack caught a break at the Final Four, played in The Pit at the University of New Mexico in Albuquerque. In the semi-finals, Phi Slama Jama, the nation's number one, faced the number-two "Doctors of Dunk" from Louisville, while State drew Georgia, a team in its first NCAA Tournament. The Wolfpack prevailed 67–60.

In the finals, N.C. State got Drexler in foul trouble and broke out to a 33–25 halftime lead. But then Houston—led by Olajuwon's 20 points, 18 rebounds, and seven blocks—went on a 17–2 run to take a 42–35 lead. Late in the game, Sidney Lowe hit a jumper to cut the Houston lead to four. Then Whittenburg sank consecutive shots to tie the score at 52 with a minute left. After Houston's Alvin Franklin missed the front end of a one-

and-one, State held the ball for the final shot. You know the rest. Drexler went for the steal, Whittenburg rushed a 30-foot airball, and Charles dunked it home. Experts said Charles never would have made the play if he hadn't been out of position. But to the untrained eye, he certainly looked like the most alert player on the floor. Those were his third and fourth points of the night. Amazingly, State had won seven of its last nine after trailing in the final minutes.

Jim Valvano is gone, having succumbed to bone cancer in 1993. Sidney Lowe coaches the Pack, which lately has been mired in the middle of the ACC. All those automobiles bearing the "Phi Packa Attacka" stickers have long since rusted away.

But as long as highlight reels run during March and April, we'll always have Lorenzo Charles' shining moment and Jimmy V storming the court, looking for a hug.

—Stephen Kirk

Big House, Billy, and the Unofficial Integration of Winston-Salem
From *They Call Me Big House*

By Clarence E. Gaines with Clint Johnson

EDITOR'S NOTE: *In the late 20th century, many people coached many sports in Winston-Salem, North Carolina, but only one of them was "The Coach": Clarence "Big House" Gaines, head men's basketball coach at historically black Winston-Salem State University. Gaines, a native of Paducah, Kentucky, had been an All-American football player at Morgan State College in Maryland. He received his nickname upon his arrival there, when an administrator got his first glimpse of the 6-foot-5-inch, 265-pound Gaines and said, "Man! The only thing I've ever seen bigger than you is a house." Gaines went to college planning to become a dentist, but after graduation his football coach recommended Gaines as an assistant to another Morgan State alum, Howard "Brutus" Wilson, who was both head football and basketball coach at what was then Winston-Salem Teachers College. Gaines was paid $1,800 a year, plus a free room in the men's dorm and discounted meals in the school cafeteria.*

When Wilson left in 1946, the school offered Gaines the job of athletic director and head coach—of football, basketball, track, tennis and boxing—trainer, and ticket manager. As men returned from World War II, however, the small college and its athletics department swelled, until Gaines was able to find new coaches for the other sports and concentrate on basketball (he once told me he chose basketball over football because a basketball team is less expensive to field, making it less vulnerable to budget cuts). He found a mentor in John McLendon, the coach at North Carolina College for Negroes (now North Carolina Central University) in Durham. McLendon had learned the game from Dr. James Naismith himself, and by the 1940s had added his own innovation to the game: the fast break.

Gaines would coach at Winston-Salem State for 47 years, earning places in the Naismith Memorial Basketball Hall of Fame, the College Basketball Hall of Fame, the CIAA Hall of Fame, and the North Carolina Sports Hall of Fame. He won eight CIAA titles and the 1967 NCAA Division II National Championship, with a team led by another Hall of Famer, future New York Knicks guard Earl Monroe. Gaines retired in 1993 as the winningest active coach in college basketball, and still stands fifth on the all-time wins list.

More impressive than his leadership inside the gym, however, was his leadership outside it. His strength of character not only helped dozens of African Americans acquire a college degree, it helped his adopted city of Winston-Salem through the end of segregation with far less strife than many other Southern cities experienced. The excerpt below, taken from Gaines' autobiography, They Call Me Big House, *written with Clint Johnson and published in 2004, the year before Gaines' death, shows how some of the first cracks began to spread through segregation, thanks to two star players and their mutual love for the game.*

☆ ☆ ☆

It was in one of the first home games of the 1959–60 season, when Cleo *[ed.—Hill, a future #1 pick in the NBA draft]* was a junior, that an event occurred that would start me, Cleo, and the city of Winston-Salem down the path to a peaceful integration of the races.

The game was just about to start when I looked up and saw a white teenager glancing around Whitaker Gym on our campus. It was easy to see him. He was the only white kid in a crowd of 2,000 black folks. Puzzled, I looked at him closer and recognized him from photos that I had seen in the *Winston-Salem Journal*'s sports section.

He was Billy Packer, a guard that Wake Forest College in Winston-Salem had recruited from a Northern high school. His father was the coach at Lehigh University in Pennsylvania.

I walked over to him, introduced myself, and said, "Son, why don't you sit down here with me, so you can ask me any questions you want?" I didn't ask him why he was there. I knew why. He was there to watch good basketball, and I needed no other explanation of what one lone white person was doing on the black side of town.

Billy sat down beside me and then asked me which of my players was Cleo Hill. News of Cleo's skills was beginning to reach a white audience, even if that audience was another college basketball player who lived and breathed the sport.

Just as I pointed to Cleo on the court, the game began. Cleo got the tip and immediately threw the ball up toward the basket—a very un-Cleo-like move. The ball never even came close to the basket. It was as big an air ball as any kid who had never played basketball could make.

Without saying a word, Billy glanced at me with maybe a touch of pity or skepticism in his eyes. I knew what he was thinking. *This is the great Cleo Hill I have been hearing so much about?* was written all over Billy's face.

But Cleo soon removed that look from Billy's face and replaced it with one of awe as he began to regularly sink 15-foot hook shots, two-handed set shots, and every other kind of shot there is in the book. Cleo was great on defense, too, even goaltending and getting away with it.

Billy didn't say much to me, but I knew exactly what he was thinking. He was thinking that the black kids in a tiny girls' college in the tiny CIAA played better basketball than the mighty North Carolina, North Carolina State, Duke, and Wake Forest in the mighty Atlantic Coast Conference.

Billy later told me that he thought the ACC probably had more overall talent spread over the entire league, and that Len Chappell, Wake's center, was better than our center. On both those counts, I would probably agree. The CIAA's smallest schools struggled to field consistently good teams, and Chappell was an excellent player.

But Billy went on to say that he had never seen

anyone like Cleo for leaping ability. Most importantly, he said the overall athleticism and speed of our team was something that he was not accustomed to seeing on white basketball courts. Without quite saying it, Billy was saying that my little Winston-Salem Teachers College team could hold their own with—if not beat—some of the big-time university teams.

The next day, Wake Forest's coach, Horace "Bones" McKinney, casually asked Billy how he had spent the previous evening.

"Watching Winston-Salem Teachers College play basketball," was Billy's reply.

Bones just nodded. He was trained to be a Baptist minister and had secretly worked behind the scenes to smooth the way for Sam Jones of North Carolina College to be drafted by the NBA in 1957. I know Bones didn't harbor any ill will toward blacks and probably didn't have any ill feelings toward anyone. Well, maybe he did have ill feelings toward the University of North Carolina at Chapel Hill, which had beaten Wake for the ACC championship in a 1957 game decided by a controversial call.

A few days later, I stopped at my office in the gym on my way to church on a Sunday morning. I heard basketballs being dribbled and shot. I would never call a practice on a Sunday morning. In fact, I urged my players to take Sunday off and go to church to get right with God.

I opened the door to the court and looked inside. There were my black players taking on the white Demon Deacons from Wake Forest in a pick-up scrimmage. There were no coaches and no fans—just a white team playing basketball against a black team. Perhaps most importantly, there were no referees and no students in street clothes acting in that role. The kids were depending on each other to call and admit to fouls.

I watched for a few seconds, then closed the door before anyone noticed me. I went on to church.

What I had witnessed was probably illegal. In most Southern towns, it was literally against the law for black athletes to play white athletes. In 1947, when Jackie Robinson had tried to play professional baseball in some Southern cities, the local governments had closed those facilities rather than allow him to play. Now, here were 20 or so black and white college students in my gym playing basketball.

Billy, without asking Coach McKinney's permission, and Cleo, without asking my permission, had arranged for the two teams to play each other whenever travel and class schedules permitted. Billy would later tell me that he had told his teammates about the phenomenal play he had seen in our game, and how the conversation had drifted around to wondering how the Wake team would perform against our players.

One thing led to another, and soon the entire white Wake team from the ritzy west side of town was regularly driving over to the poor east side of town to scrimmage. Sometimes, my black players would cram themselves into a couple of cars and make the trip over to Wake.

Dozens of these unauthorized scrimmages occurred in the early to the mid-1960s, thanks to Billy Packer, who started them as a player and then continued them when he graduated and returned a few years later as a Wake Forest assistant coach.

What Billy and his teammates and Cleo and his teammates did was unofficially integrate Winston-Salem. According to Billy and Cleo, there was never any conflict between the two races on the basketball court. There were no racial taunts, no macho displays, no fistfights, no violence of any kind. Coach McKinney and I wouldn't know. We were never invited to attend any of those scrimmages. I don't think a single one of them was ever supervised or even witnessed for the full game by a coach on either team. This was the players' idea, and I think both coaches instinctively knew that it should stay their idea.

In one sense, those scrimmages were amazing. In 1959, in a South where racial segregation was the social and legal norm, there were 20 or so black and white young men slamming into each other on a court in an intense basketball game. Despite all this physical contact, there was no violence.

. . . I don't think the newspaper editors ever got wind of the scrimmages. If they did, they chose not to send reporters to cover them. I know the police never got wind of the games. If they had, they might have sent a squad over to break them up, and maybe even to arrest me for knowingly allowing the races to mix on the basketball court. The games remained a secret known mostly to the players themselves.

Billy went on to do pretty well for himself. After leaving coaching, he became a college basketball play-by-play announcer for television. I remember watching Billy on his first college broadcast, a game between Maryland and North Carolina in Chapel Hill. Billy was interviewing Maryland coach Lefty Driesell when he made some kind of comment about how "we don't think much of you down here in North Carolina." Lefty just stared at him, not sure what to say.

I knew what to say. Billy tells me that no television executive called him up to critique his first performance, but I did. I told Billy just one thing and then hung up: "Don't ever insult a coach to his face to get a reaction."

Billy's done much better since that rocky night. I think he is one of the best college-sports commentators working on network television today. I call him one of my millionaire friends.

Charlotte Hornets

Praise them or curse them for it, the Charlotte Hornets brought teal into the public consciousness. Moreover, they were so bold—or so reckless—as to pair it with purple. Even the folks at Crayola took notice, adding a teal crayon to their line.

Luck smiled on the Hornets early. They joined the NBA with the Miami Heat in 1988, a year ahead of the Orlando Magic and the Minnesota Timberwolves. The timing was perfect. Charlotte, a banking center on the rise, was itching to declare itself a major league city.

Hornets owner George Shinn was the toast of the Carolinas. As a 20-year-old, Shinn had arranged with Evans Business College in Concord, north of Charlotte, to do janitorial labor to help pay his tuition. One day while working, he saw two girls rattling the door. He showed them around and gave them application materials. The next day, the school's director called him out of class and said that four girls were interested in enrolling and wanted to talk to Mr. Shinn. Subsequently hired by the school as a recruiter, he brought in more students than the rest of the staff combined, though still studying full time. He bought a portion of the school, then the whole school, then similar business schools, putting together a 30-campus empire, the Rutledge Education System. After cashing out for $30 million in the early 1980s, he got into real estate, publishing, car dealerships, and sports teams. At various times, he owned the Charlotte Knights and Gastonia Rangers baseball teams, the Charlotte Checkers hockey team, and the Charlotte Sting women's basketball team, in addition to the Hornets. His rags-to-riches ascent made him the youngest-ever winner of the Horatio Alger Award.

His Hornets, more inclined toward veteran castoffs than youngsters, were as bad as expected for an expansion franchise, winning 20 games against 62 losses. But that hardly mattered to the fans. The Hive, as the Charlotte Coliseum was coming to be known, was indeed alive. The Hornets led the NBA in attendance, outdrawing second-place Detroit, the eventual champion on the court, by 70,000. Their total attendance of 950,064 exceeded the league average by over 50 percent. Forward Kelly Tripucka had a great year, averaging 22.6 points. But fans identified most closely with Tyrone "Muggsy" Bogues, at 5-foot-3 the smallest player in NBA history. The "Little Engine That Could" in short pants, Bogues personified a team that had to overachieve to win. Fans at the packed Hive were well satisfied with spirited losses.

The Hornets' next two seasons followed the same script, the team going 19–63 and 26–56 and continuing its string of last-place divisional finishes.

Then came the greatest good fortune in Charlotte Hornets history. The team had finished the previous year with the fifth-worst record in the league and went into the 1991 draft lottery with a 10.61 percent chance of landing the top pick. But the Hornets won the big prize—the rights to UNLV forward Larry Johnson, the consensus top player in college. The following year, they entered the lottery with the eighth-worst record, 31–51, but beat the odds again to win the second overall pick, with which they selected Georgetown center Alonzo Mourning, a player good enough to be at the top of the board most years.

Suddenly, a ragtag franchise had two players around whom to build a title contender. The 1992–93 Hornets won nine of their last 12 to finish 44–38 and reach the playoffs for the first time. They faced Boston, led by rising star Reggie Lewis, the first Celtics captain after Larry Bird and a former high-school teammate of Bogues. During the opening contest, Lewis collapsed on Boston's parquet floor, the victim of a heart defect. He never played again and died three months later. The Hornets lost that first game but went on to beat the dispirited Celtics in four, Mourning taking them into the second round with a dramatic buzzer-beater in Charlotte.

That shot—after which Mourning fell flat on his back on the court in celebration—was the Charlotte Hornets' high-water mark. They lost to the Knicks in five games in the second round. The following season, they missed the playoffs after Johnson injured his back and Mourning had leg problems. In 1994–95, they posted a 50–32 record but had the misfortune to run into Michael Jordan —newly back from his hiatus playing baseball—in the first round of the post-season.

The next year was marked by disastrous personnel moves. The team initially retained Johnson—never the same player after his back trouble—but Shinn wouldn't pay what was necessary to keep Mourning, who was traded to Miami in a blockbuster deal for Glen Rice and others. Then the Hornets traded away the draft rights to Kobe Bryant and also traded Johnson to New York.

Shinn's tight wallet wasn't the only reason the bloom was off the rose in Charlotte. In 1997, a woman accused him of forcing her to give him oral sex. Two years later, the woman's civil suit against Shinn was broadcast nationally on Court TV. During the proceedings, a pair of former employees claimed Shinn had sexually harassed them, and he admitted to an extramarital affair with, among others, a Hornets dance team member. Not long before the team came into being, Charlotteans had witnessed the circus surrounding the sexual misdoings of another super-religious figure, Jim Bakker. They were not amused by Shinn's troubles.

Meanwhile, the new-look Hornets had some successes, though they never again found cornerstones like Johnson and Mourning. Glen Rice averaged 26.8 points in 1996–97 and scored 20 points in one quarter in the All Star game, a record. The following season, the team finished 51–31 and reached the second round of the playoffs, losing to Chicago. A low point came in the 1999–2000 season when popular guard Bobby Phills was killed while racing cars with teammate David Wesley after practice. The Hornets regrouped the next year behind new star Baron Davis to make the playoffs' second round for the third time in franchise history, falling to Milwaukee in seven games.

Despite that success, the Hive was no longer buzzing. Attendance was near the bottom of the league. The fans were thoroughly disillusioned with Shinn, who was demanding taxpayer money for a new building, though the Charlotte Coliseum was little more than 10 years old. City leaders were inclined to provide those funds under one condition—that Shinn sell the team to someone else. Anyone else.

The man once feted with a ticker-tape parade in Charlotte and a George Shinn Day in two states was now a pariah. When he opted to move the Hornets to New Orleans for the 2002–3 season, more than a few fans hoped the door would indeed hit him on the way out.

—STEPHEN KIRK

Mountaineers Bring Down the Big House

From *King of the Mountain: The Jerry Moore Story*

By Dick Brown

Jerry: When Charlie [Cobb, the ASU athletic director] came down to my office to tell me of the possibility of playing Michigan, I jumped at it. He came back several times after that to make sure I really wanted to play a Big 10 powerhouse like Michigan. I told him absolutely, with no hesitation. It would be a great experience for our team and give our program a lot of good exposure. After we looked at the tapes that summer before spring ball, I told the other coaches that I believed we could play with those guys.

One day, getting dressed out for spring practice, our quarterback, Armanti Edwards, came up to me and asked if we were really going to play Michigan. I told him not to worry; they put their pants on one leg at a time just like he did. He looked at me, and said, "But coach, they wear 48 longs!"

We all laughed, but I was serious. I felt like we had the talent to stay in the game with them. The team proved on the field what I felt all along, with one of the biggest upsets in football history. After that game and all the notoriety, we had a target on our backs so big you could see it a mile away. Everybody was gunning for us.

Margaret: When Jerry came home that day last spring and said, "Margaret, how would you like to go to the Big House?" I answered, "Sure, that would be great. Are you talking about the White House in Washington, D.C.?"

He said, "No, I'm talking about the University of Michigan. That's what they call their stadium. It holds 109,000 people and we are going to play them there our first game."

Editor's Note: Texas-born Jerry Moore became the head football coach at Appalachian State University in Boone, North Carolina, in 1989. He came to the Mountaineers after an up-and-down, well-traveled coaching career. He was an assistant coach under Hayden Fry at Southern Methodist University, Tom Osborne at Nebraska, and Ken Hatfield at Arkansas, and was head coach at North Texas and Texas Tech. After a career spent mostly at major programs in NCAA Division 1A (now the Football Bowl Subdivision), coming to Appalachian, a Football Championship Subdivision program (because their champions are determined in a playoff, not by voters), might have been considered a step down. Moore, however, not only became the all-time winningest coach in the Southern Conference, he turned the Mountaineers into one of the most respected football teams in the nation—largely because of the game described in this excerpt from Dick Brown's 2008 book *King of the Mountain: The Jerry Moore Story*, which includes extensive comments from Coach Moore and his wife, Margaret.

He was so excited about playing a really great team in front of that many people, I couldn't believe it. He said they would be a top-ranked team and they packed that big stadium every home game. Who would have thought we would beat them in their own stadium? It was really an emotional game. My hands were shaking so bad I couldn't hold my binoculars still on that last play when Corey blocked their field-goal try.

It was such a big upset with all the national coverage. I really felt sorry for Coach Lloyd Carr's wife after the game. I understood how she must have felt. Just knowing what was going on here in Boone, I can only imagine what was going on up there. We knocked them completely out of the national ratings; that must have been tough to take. I sat down and wrote her a letter as soon as we got home.

With two straight national championships under their belt, and 13 starters—10 of them seniors—returning for the 2007 season, Boone was all abuzz with excitement. Walking in downtown Boone on King Street, black-and-gold Appalachian T-shirts and bumper stickers were everywhere. Coach Moore said a man came up to him and held up two tickets to the Michigan game.

Jerry: *I'd like to have a nickel for every time I heard the term "three-peat" before the season even started. Everybody was asking if we were going to three-peat when I went anywhere. Just walking around town or at the grocery store, no matter where I went, everybody asked.*

When asked if he minded all the talk about a three-peat, Coach Moore said, "Shoot no, everybody was just excited to get the season started, and so were we. A lot of people talked about the national attention that winning the championships brought to our school. That's a neat thing to experience here in Boone. People really wanted to identify with our team."

Moore's program had been good for a long time; 17 of his 18 teams had winning records. The previous two years, the Mountaineers blossomed into back-to-back national champions. In spite of what some of his detractors said back in 2004, Jerry Moore's coaching had only gotten better. The loyal coaching staff had been around an average of nine years, except for defense coordinator John Wiley, who came up with Moore from Texas in 1989.

This was a new season, however, with three of their four down linemen graduated off the two-championship defense. Returning were record-setting and All-Conference quarterback Armanti Edwards along with All-Conference and ASU record-breaking Kevin Richardson at tailback. Seven starters on offense and six on defense would return.

Moore and his staff were challenged to fill in where there were holes. As usual, Moore had a stable of talented freshmen and sophomores, waiting for their chance to make the starting team. Their goal was the same as the veterans: return to Chattanooga for an unprecedented third national championship.

Senior All-Conference center Scott Suttle said it best: "It's an even bigger bull's-eye on us this year, but I think we're expecting even more of ourselves."

When September 1 rolled around, it was time to put away all the talk of the last two championships. The Mountaineers were going to the Big House. The University of Michigan's gargantuan stadium was the largest football stadium in the country, and it was sold out every home game to watch the winningest program in college football.

Jerry: *Yeah, they were big and fast and have probably the longest winning tradition in college football. But we have a winning tradition, too, and we prepare the same way we do every week and every year for each team we play. We usually keep the team together the night before a game and watch an inspirational movie. We planned to watch the "Miracle on Ice" movie about the American Olympic hockey team that beat the Russians that we watched before playing Northern Iowa and UMass for the championships.*

We had our projectionist rig it up so the beginning of the Miracle *movie would start first. You could hear the guys, especially the seniors, groan a little. Then the movie* Invincible *came on. They cheered. It's a true story about thirty-year-old Vince Papale who was down on his luck as a part-time teacher and part-time bartender who made it as a walk-on for the Philadelphia Eagles. What are the odds of that happening in the NFL? But we have a history of successful walk-ons. There were four starters and All-Conference players that played for us as walkons. They could really identify with the movie and really enjoyed it.*

Inspirational movies and speakers are just some of the ways we try to help our players get their feet on the ground and mentor them. Another thing the players have done under the leadership of Nic Cardwell, Corey Lynch, and Billy Riddell, before he left on a mission trip to Africa, was to form a weekly Bible study. We don't preach at the guys or anything like that, but we are here as role models for these young men.

We form a voluntary prayer circle holding hands before each game. We are trying to help build successful student athletes and young men of character so when they get out in the world they will be prepared for whatever comes up. I can't say that we have ever had divine intervention in any of our games, as some newspapers have, but it sure doesn't hurt to try.

Michigan had never played a lower Division I FCS team before, but Coach Lloyd Carr didn't see any risk in playing Appalachian. The Wolverines had won 11 consecutive games the previous season and were picked fifth in the pre-season poll.

"We had the benefit of watching all of Appalachian's games from last fall," Michigan Coach Carr said. "We knew their strengths from the standpoint of their speed and integrating a great athlete at quarterback who was a threat and who touches the ball on every play."

More than 20,000 black-and-gold-clad fans poured into the Big House for the long-awaited start of the next assault on a third championship. The players looked like ants running around the field to the visitors in the upper sections, but the fans were proud to be there to make some noise for the Mountaineers.

Jerry: *I got chills coming out of the tunnel and trotting on to the field in front of all those people and hearing our fans cheering for us. I've never seen anything like it; it was awesome. That was an experience I will remember the rest of my life. And for some of our freshmen, who were playing high-school ball this time last year, it was beyond anything they could have ever imagined.*

The Teams 51

MARGARET: *We were pretty far up and had to use binoculars to see the guys. But they didn't look excited at all. They were so calm as they went through their warm-up drills. I think Jerry was more nervous than they were. I wasn't nervous until the Michigan team came out. They were huge and they just kept coming out of that tunnel. Then I got nervous.*

Michigan scored on their opening drive, but the Mountaineers weren't intimidated. Appalachian came right back on its first possession and showcased its speed as Dexter Jackson gathered in a short pass over the middle and turned it into a 68-yard touchdown. The Wolverines held Appalachian in check the rest of the first quarter. But the Mountaineers went on a three-touchdown rampage in the second quarter and shut Michigan out until the last 16 seconds before the half when the Wolverines managed a field goal to make it 28–17.

The reality of the speed and skills of Appalachian began to sink in to a stunned Michigan team as they headed to the dressing room. While the score was still 28–14, a Michigan security guard on the sidelines turned to Randy Jackson, WKBC sideline reporter and the father of ASU play-by-play announcer David Jackson, and asked, "Didn't your guys get the memo? You're not supposed to win."

The second half saw Michigan make a big comeback against the tiring Mountaineers, who only used 35 players the entire game. Julian Rauch's field goal kept the Mountaineers in the lead until late in the fourth quarter. A pair of Michigan touchdowns nudged the Wolverines into the lead, 32–31, after the Mountaineer defense denied both of Michigan's two-point conversion attempts.

The Mountaineer offense stepped it up a notch. They fought their way down to a first and goal on the Michigan five-yard line with 30 seconds left and no timeouts. Coach Moore decided to go for the field goal rather than risk a turnover or run out of time. Rauch's 24-yard kick split the uprights for a 34–32 lead.

In their hurry-up 30-second drill after the kickoff, Michigan's Heisman candidate, Chad Henne, completed a 46-yard pass to the Mountaineers' 20-yard line. With only six seconds showing on the clock the Wolverines lined up for a field-goal attempt. It was a 37-yard attempt, well within their kicker's range.

All-American safety Corey Lynch lined up wide outside the left side of the Michigan line. On the snap of the ball, Lynch streaked in untouched and blocked the kick with his chest. The ball took an Appalachian bounce and Lynch quickly scooped the ball up in stride and headed for Michigan's goal line. Fatigue and leg cramps slowed the league-leading kick blocker down and he was shoved out of bounds on the five-yard line as time expired.

"It sounded like a volcano erupting on our sideline when Corey blocked that kick and picked it up to try and score," Moore said. Then pandemonium broke out from the 20,000-plus Appalachian fans who poured down from the stadium onto the playing field as nearly 90,000 Michigan fans stood in shocked silence. There was jubilation all over the field as reporters swarmed around the Mountaineers.

"I really wanted to score at the Big House," said the game's hero Corey Lynch. He joked about the late-game heroics and said, "That's our plan every game to keep App State fans interested." They had managed to do that almost every week the previous two seasons. Later, when asked if he thought that the win over No. 5–ranked Michigan should get the Mountaineers ranked in the Division I FBS polls, Lynch said, "I think we just proved it today." Lynch was proven correct as the FBS voted to change their rules to include FCS teams in their rankings two days after the big upset. The rule became known as the "Appalachian State Rule." And the Mountaineers enjoyed a brief FBS ranking in the top 25.

The monster win brought a media blitz to Boone like none other. Immediately after the game, celebrating students stormed Kidd Brewer stadium, took down a goal post, and paraded it around campus. When the bus arrived from the Tri-Cities airport, a crowd of 10,000 students and fans, still celebrating, were gathered at Kidd Brewer Stadium to greet their giant-slayers.

The High Country's *Watauga Democrat* ran a special edition—"The Anatomy of an Upset"—loaded with photos of the game and celebrating students carrying a goal post down the street on campus. The *Winston-Salem Journal's* "Mountaineers Win One for the Ages" ran atop Sunday's sports page. The greatest national recognition of the Mountaineers' feat was the *Sports Illustrated* story and cover photo of Dexter Jackson streaking for a touchdown with the title "Alltime Upset: Appalachian State Stuns No. 5 Michigan."

Issues of the magazine flew off the shelves everywhere in the High Country and the rest of western North Carolina. Local fans were forced to call relatives in other states to get copies of the upset of all time. Coach Moore was said to have a big stack of *Sports Illustrated* magazines on his desk to sign for proud fans. His secretary, Denise, indicated it would probably be Christmas break before he could get them all signed.

"The Greatest College Sports Program Ever"

As much success as Roy Williams has had as head coach of the University of North Carolina men's basketball team, he has a long way to go to catch Anson Dorrance.

Williams won the 2005 NCAA Championship, the Tar Heels' fifth national title in basketball.

The UNC women's soccer team has won 19 national titles under Dorrance, who had won 648 games going into the 2008 season, his 30th as head coach of the Tar Heels. UNC produced the world's most famous basketball player, Michael Jordan, but the school also produced the world's most famous female soccer player, Mia Hamm. As of 2007, UNC women's soccer rosters included 66 players named first-team All-Americans, more than twice as many as any other school. UNC players had been named National Player of the Year 17 times. The United States' winning entry to the first Women's World Cup, in 1991, included nine former Tar Heels players and Dorrance as coach; subsequent World Cup and Olympic teams have never fielded fewer than four UNC alumna. In 2003, *Sports Illustrated on Campus* magazine called UNC women's soccer "the greatest college sports program ever."

Dorrance was born in 1951 in Bombay, India. His father, an oil executive, kept the family on the move throughout Dorrance's youth, spending time in Ethiopia, Kenya, Singapore, Belgium, and Switzerland. Soccer was one constant. Dorrance became a three-time All-ACC soccer player at Carolina, graduating in 1974. He spent two years organizing youth soccer leagues after graduation, before returning in 1976 as coach of the men's soccer team.

UNC did not have a varsity women's soccer team until 1979, when Dorrance was named its first and, so far, only head coach. He continued to coach both the men's and women's teams until 1989, winning national coach of the year honors as men's coach in 1987, and as women's coach in 1982, 1986, 1997, 2000, 2003, and 2006. He was inducted into the North Carolina Sports Hall of Fame in 2005, and into the National Soccer Hall of Fame in 2008.

UNC won its first national title in 1981, only three years after the program was formed. They won the next three national championships in a row, before losing in the 1985 finals. That loss, 2–0 to George Mason, was their last of the decade: from the start of the 1986 season, the Tar Heels won 97 and tied six of their next 103 games. Their streak was snapped in 1990, in overtime at Connecticut; the Tar Heels got the Huskies back by beating them 6–0 in the national finals. Dorrance and UNC followed that up by winning 92 games in a row, before tying Notre Dame and losing to Duke (after beating the Blue Devils 101 straight times) during the 1994 season. Along the way, UNC won nine straight national championships.

The biggest threat to UNC's dominance of women's soccer came not from an opponent on the field, but from a sexual harassment lawsuit filed against Dorrance by a player he had cut. The lawsuit was dismissed by a federal appeals court in 2006, with the majority opinion stating that "Dorrance never touched, never threatened, never ogled, and never propositioned" the plaintiff, adding that "no reasonable jury could find that Dorrance sexually harassed" her.

Soccer aficionados say Dorrance's success has less to do with technical or tactical coaching than with his ability to motivate female athletes, particularly early in his career, when many still considered "female athletes" something of an oxymoron. Hamm said it best in a 1998 *Sports Illustrated* article: "I grew up always good at sports, but being a girl, I was never allowed to feel as good about it as guys were. My toughness wasn't celebrated. But then I came here, and it was O.K. to want to be the best."

—ED SOUTHERN

Proud to be a Deacon

By Ed Southern

Wake Forest fans find themselves living in strange days.

As I write this, the Wake Forest men's basketball team is ranked number one in the country, and was the last unbeaten team in NCAA Division I. Last week's loss to Virginia Tech will have probably cost them their top ranking when the new polls come out, but they remain a serious contender for the Final Four, if not the NCAA championship (and as I wrote that, I knocked on wood so hard my knuckles almost bled).

Wake fans are not used to pulling for the number one team in the country in a major sport. We're used to rooting for the plucky underdog. We're used to *being* the underdog, at least in terms of numbers. The 4,412 undergraduates currently enrolled at Wake make up the smallest student body in the major NCAA conferences—and the largest student body in Wake Forest history. When I graduated from Wake 15 years ago, I was one of only about 2,800 undergrads. I once heard (I won't bother to verify this, because it's too good an anecdote to risk being disproved, and it's true spiritually if not factually) that schools like Ohio State and Michigan have more students enrolled than Wake Forest has living alumni.

We tend to be nice, too, maybe because of the school's Baptist heritage, or maybe because we're so outnumbered and we are, generally speaking, not stupid (more on that later). Will Blythe, author of *To Hate Like This Is to Be Happy Forever: A Thoroughly Obsessive, Intermittently Uplifting, and Occasionally Unbiased Account of the Duke-North Carolina Basketball Rivalry*, calls Wake Forest "everybody's second-favorite ACC team." Wake has no true rival. Wake fans get especially excited anytime we play the University of North Carolina; UNC fans think of the next Wake game just as the next game. The superstars who have come out of Wake are usually seen as paragons of decency and humility, athletes who are hard to hate: Brian Piccolo (who was not a superstar on the field, but was the subject of the movie *Brian's Song*), Arnold Palmer, Tim Duncan, Chris Paul (unless you happen to be Julius Hodge). Mark Packer, host of the syndicated radio show "Primetime with the Packman" (and son of former Wake star Billy Packer), calls Wake Forest "Switzerland," because it's a pretty place with pleasant people whom no one really hates.

Having one of the best basketball teams in the nation, while hardly a regular expectation, is not a complete shock to the Wake fan's system. Wake, despite some down years, is usually at least a second-tier power in college basketball. During his sophomore year, Chris Paul led Wake to two weeks atop the rankings and a regular-season ACC title. Tim Duncan won back-to-back ACC Tournaments, the first one as a supporting player to Randolph Childress, the second one practically on his own. Wake's happy little secret is that in basketball and almost all other sports, our teams have always been respectable, if not downright great. The men's soccer team won the 2007 national championship, and made it to the 2008 College Cup. The baseball team is only a few years removed from their own back-to-back ACC titles. The women's field hockey team is virtually a dynasty, having won three straight national championships from 2002–2004 and appearing in the NCAA semi-finals or finals every year since. The track, cross country, and tennis teams regularly produce All-Americans and even Olympians, and the men's golf team—with an alumni roster that includes Palmer, Curtis Strange, Billy Andrade, Jay Haas, and Lanny Wadkins—chases titles year-in and year-out.

In fact, the only sport in which Wake Forest has no tradition of achievement, the only sport in which opponents could regularly and justifiably take the Demon Deacons lightly, the sport in which Wake earned its reputation as plucky but harmless, is the only sport that really matters to most of the South and the nation.

Historically, Wake Forest has sucked at football.

But take note of how I began that last sentence. Take note of that word "historically," because in the last few years, Wake Forest football has become a program to be respected, maybe even feared.

Frankly, Wake fans still aren't quite sure how to handle that. Strange days, indeed.

☆ ☆ ☆

Wake Forest hired Jim Grobe as its head football coach in December 2000. The West Virginian, an Academic All-ACC player at the University of Virginia, came to Wake from the head coaching job at Ohio University, where his 33–33–1 record was impressive but hardly awe-inspiring. That was in line with previous Wake coaching hires, at least in football. Being the head coach of the Wake Forest football team had been, at best, a stepping stone; at worst, a stone around the neck of a coach's career record. In a July 2008 column, CBSSportsline.com's Gregg Doyel called the position "that one-time joke of a job," saying, "Put it this way: The Indianapolis Colts are committed to promoting assistant coach Jim Caldwell whenever Tony Dungy steps down [Dungy stepped down in January 2009, and Caldwell was promoted], despite Caldwell's horrific career record of 26–63 at Wake Forest. Or this way: Al Groh got the New York Jets job in 2000, and the Virginia job in '01, despite going 26–40 at Wake Forest. Good coaches fail at Wake Forest. Everyone understands."

Realistic Wake fans understood, too. We would have been pleased if this new guy Grobe could get 6 or 7 wins a season, maybe make an obscure bowl game every few years. We also understood that if he won more than that, he'd soon be gone to a better job at a bigger school.

The win-loss record stayed typically Wake Forest during Grobe's first five years—6–5, 7–6, 5–7, and 4–7 twice. To an outsider looking only at the bottom line and not the games, or to someone who watched the games but didn't know much about football, nothing about the Wake program had changed with Grobe's hiring.

To the fans, reporters, and opponents who watched the team, saw the little things, and understood what they'd seen, the 21st-century Demon Deacons looked nothing like the Deacons of old. Wake's small size, high academic standards, limited resources, and lack of tradition still—and probably always will—put them at a disadvantage in overall athletic ability and depth, but they no longer played as if they knew they were at a disadvantage. They played, simultaneously, with more discipline and more ferocity: sticking to their assignments, executing complex pulls and stunts on the line, hitting harder.

Grobe and his staff insisted on redshirting almost every freshman who arrived, sacrificing immediate results for the delayed gratification of an extra season of practice. They also seemed to be the first coaches to take what had long been seen as a Wake Forest weakness—the high academic standards required of its students, even its student-athletes—and turn it into a strength. The Wake offense made up for its relative lack of size and speed with smarts, employing Grobe's hallmark "flexbone" offense—a staggering variety of sets and looks, lining up one down in what looked like a spread formation, the next in what looked like a standard I-back set, the next in what looked like an option. They regularly used what most teams would consider trick plays, including the soon-famous "Orbit Sweep," in which a receiver in motion receives a pitch just after passing the quarterback, confusing (one hopes) the defense and getting the ball around the edge that much sooner.

Grobe had given clues, beyond the usual coach-speak of press conferences and banquet speeches, that change was coming to Wake Forest football. The August after Grobe's hiring, Winston-Salem's NBC affiliate replaced a vacationing weatherman with a different local celebrity each day on its morning news. Grobe took his turn on a day that promised a particular swelter. After reading the standard warning about high ozone levels and avoiding exertion outdoors, he then added his own comment: "Unless you're one of my players. In that case, you'd better expect to work."

☆ ☆ ☆

At the start of the 2006 season, Grobe's Wake Forest winning percentage was less than .500, but optimism surrounding the program was high enough to allow the university to begin a six-stage renovation of its home field, Groves Stadium, now known as BB&T Field. Attendance grew steadily, with the Deacons setting what was then a single-game attendance record for the 2004 UNC match. Fans had high expectations for 2006, the first season in which highly touted quarterback Ben Mauk would be the undisputed starter.

In the third quarter of the first game, against Syracuse, Mauk dove to recover a fumble, stretching his throwing arm out in front of him to gather the ball. Two Orangemen defenders landed on top of his outstretched arm and shoulder, breaking his upper arm, tearing his labrum, and dislocating his shoulder. He was wheeled off the field on a stretcher, his season done. Most fans at the game that day didn't even know the name of Mauk's backup.

His name, in fact, was Brett Hodges, but as it turned out, Hodges was recovering himself from a minor injury. Redshirt freshman Riley Skinner, the third-string quarterback, took over behind center.

The starting quarterback is almost always the face of a football team, but Skinner came to be the symbol of both the 2006 season and the program under Jim

Grobe. No player could have been more unheralded; he had been the last player in his class to be offered a scholarship, and that offer had come almost as an afterthought. No player's—and no team's—success that year could have been less expected. Skinner, like his team (with a few exceptions), is not blessed with extraordinary size or athletic ability, but he plays with intelligence and poise, plays "within himself," as coaches and commentators like to say, and he does what is needed to win. Like his coach, he is just demonstrative enough to get the point across; he stays calm, seems humble, and is not given to histrionics on the sideline or in the huddle.

Those character traits are perhaps what most endear Grobe and his staff to Wake Forest fans (those, and his coaching ability). Grobe coaches in what could be called "the Wake Forest Way," if the Wake Forest Way didn't include too much modesty to call itself the Wake Forest Way. By all accounts, including his own, Grobe appreciates and enjoys the small size, the collegial campus, the academic rigor of the school. One of his least favorite but most-used words is "knucklehead," as in the kind of player he does not want to recruit. One of his favorite words is "salty," as in perhaps not spectacular, but seasoned, experienced, smart, gritty. The 2006 defense was extra salty, except on those occasions when they were spectacular. Great teams are usually defined and remembered by game-winning drives and scores; Wake's 2006 team was defined by game-winning defense. They had a knack for letting an opponent drive almost the length of the field, then coming up with an interception (often in the end zone) or forced fumble that sealed the victory. That defense, and the uncannily accurate foot of kicker Sam Swank, had more to do with what happened in 2006 than Wake's offense, even if Riley Skinner became the hero and the symbol.

Skinner entered the Syracuse game and led the drive that scored the winning points. He stayed in the starting lineup and led Wake to wins in their first five games, only the third time Wake had begun a season 5–0. He led Wake back after a heartbreaking loss to Clemson. He led Wake Forest to nine wins for the first time in school history, then led them to two more; he led Wake to an AP Top 25 ranking, led Wake Forest—little ol' Wake Forest—to the ACC Championship and the Orange Bowl, winning the ACC Rookie of the Year award along the way.

Wake Forest, football champions of the ACC, standing atop the conference that includes Florida State, the University of Miami, Virginia Tech. Wake Forest, smallest school in the BCS conferences. Wake Forest, whose most famous football player, Brian Piccolo, is famous for having died early, bravely, and tragically.

By the way, Winston-Salem felt the tremors of an earthquake that year. I'm not sayin'; I'm just sayin'.

☆ ☆ ☆

More difficult for the lifelong Wake Forest fan to grasp was that the 2006 season was not a fluke, a one-off, a magical season in which all the stars aligned and our team did something preposterous. Most of Wake Forest's past success came during years in which a particularly talented and cohesive class of seniors came together, clicked, and won more games than expected. Then those seniors graduated, and perhaps the coach moved on to bigger and better things, and Wake Forest would struggle the next year to four wins. A year after winning 11 games, Wake Forest won 9. The next year, Wake Forest won 8, including its second bowl win in a row, the first time Wake Forest has ever won back-to-back bowls, not to mention the first time Wake has ever gone to three bowl games in three straight years—and Wake football fans were *disappointed*, after starting the season as the ACC's last undefeated team, picked by many to win the conference again. The football players in the Class of 2009 are the winningest group in school history, and Riley Skinner—with one more season to go—is Wake's all-time winningest quarterback.

To the shock and delight of fans, and the shock of college football observers, Jim Grobe is still the head coach at Wake after eight years, numberless rumors, and at least a few solid job offers. He won't rule out the possibility of his leaving for another job—and at some level, even the most fanatical Demon Deacon couldn't blame him—but he has repeatedly said that it would have to be the perfect opportunity, since he's very happy at little ol' Wake Forest.

Wake Forest football games have changed off the field as well as on. For 2008 Wake Forest opened Deacon Tower, a brand-new, state-of-the-art facility that replaced the press and luxury boxes that had been in place since the stadium opened in the late 1960s. The exterior and grounds of BB&T Field were renovated and re-landscaped, adding bricks and arches that match the ones with which the campus is built. Athletic Director Ron Wellman's stated reasoning behind the changes was that while Wake could never have the biggest stadium in college football, they could have the nicest.

Long gone are the days when a fan could drive over to the stadium a half-hour before game time, walk up to the ticket window with little or no wait, buy a ticket, then sit almost anywhere he wanted, since vast gaps in seating would be available at almost any game. Sellouts are common now, parking is hard to come by. People from the Winston-Salem area, with no prior allegiance to Wake Forest, have jumped on the bandwagon. A little fan education is still in order—the scoreboard and PA still remind fans to make noise when the opponent has the ball on third down, and they *need to* remind fans not to make noise when Wake has the ball on third down—but the energy, the rowdiness, the fanatical part of being a fan is in place.

Strange days, indeed.

The Carolina Panthers

It didn't matter that Jake Delhomme made the NFL the hard way. Or that he always faced criticism manfully. Or that he'd led the team to a Super Bowl. Or that he'd come back after having his elbow reassembled.

When Delhomme reached halftime of the Carolina Panthers' 2009 playoff debacle against Arizona with a quarterback rating (13.9) that would make Chris Weinke blush, and ultimately finished with five interceptions and a fumble, he understood that radio and Internet invective was coming. He heard the boos and saw people walking out of Bank of America Stadium.

In the short term, Delhomme was lucky to have Jerry Richardson and John Fox behind him. Richardson, awaiting a heart transplant, was watching from his box. A former 13th-round pick and the first ex-NFL player to own a team since George Halas, he had a perspective on the game unique among his peers. And Fox, always the first to congratulate and the last to criticize his players, kept his composure through Delhomme's many mistakes. "We picked a bad day to have a bad day" was the strongest post-game comment the coach made.

But don't be fooled. Panthers management will upgrade at quarterback—and any other position—in a heartbeat. That's life in the NFL. Everything is magnified in a league that denotes its championships with Roman numerals. The season is shorter than in other sports, each game more critical. The stadiums and TV audiences are larger. The hits are brutal and the injuries sometimes lifelong. Citizen-experts are legion and vocal.

The Charlotte Bobcats have no fan base. The Carolina Hurricanes inhabit an iffy market in a struggling league. The Panthers are without doubt the Cadillac pro franchise in the Carolinas.

Jerry Richardson used his $3,500 check from the 1959 NFL playoffs—in which he caught the championship-winning pass from Johnny Unitas—to found Spartan Foods, which had interests in Hardee's restaurants and steakhouse and seafood chains. In the late 1980s, following the announcement that Charlotte would get an NBA franchise, Richardson began lobbying for an NFL team. In June 1993, he revealed plans to finance a stadium through the sale of personal seat licenses, rather than taxpayer money. Fans bought all the seats by the end of the day they went on sale.

The Panthers and the Jacksonville Jaguars joined the league in 1995. Both benefited from a wrinkle not available to previous newcomers—free agency. Among the Panthers' significant acquisitions their inaugural year were top draft pick Kerry Collins and free agents John Kasay and Sam Mills. The first player they ever cut? Bill Goldberg. Football's loss proved to be wrestling's gain. The Panthers put together a surprising 7–9 record, including a four-game winning streak and a victory over defending champ San Francisco. Since their stadium was under construction, they played home games in Death Valley at Clemson University, briefly becoming the only major league sports team ever based in South Carolina.

In 1996, both the Panthers and Jacksonville reached their conference title games. Carolina in the NFC. The Panthers rode Collins, Kasay, Mills, Kevin Greene, Wesley Walls, Eric Davis, and rookie Muhsin Muhammad to a 12–4 record and a first-round playoff win over Dallas before falling 30–13 to Green Bay.

Following that swift ascent, the Panthers fell to 7–9 and 4–12 the next two seasons. Original coach Dom Capers was replaced by George Seifert, a two-time champion with the 49ers. Seifert set about proving what his critics had always said—that he couldn't win without inherited talent like he had in San Francisco. After he led them to 8–8 and 7–9 seasons in 1999 and 2000, respectively, the Panthers bottomed out in 2001, winning their opener before losing 15 straight behind overwhelmed rookie quarterback Weinke. Seifert was fired.

Off the field, things were just as bad. Kerry Collins became an alcoholic and made racial comments about teammates. The Panthers released him in 1998. The following year, receiver Rae Carruth conspired to murder his pregnant girlfriend, blocking her vehicle while another man pumped four bullets into her. Carruth was apprehended hiding in a car trunk at a Tennessee motel. In 2000, recently traded running back Fred Lane was shot dead by his wife at their Charlotte home.

Those incidents plus bad personnel moves like the acquisition of defensive tackle Sean Gilbert put the Panthers at a crossroads. Fans wondered if they were becoming a dysfunctional franchise.

The team's flirtation with high-priced Steve Spurrier as Seifert's replacement provided little reassurance. The Panthers' second choice, Tony Dungy, turned them down, too. And so John Fox, the Giants' defensive coordinator, got his chance.

In the draft, the Panthers added number-two overall pick Julius Peppers to a defense that included Dan Morgan, Kris Jenkins, Mike Rucker, and Mike Minter. They improved to 7–9 in 2002 and claimed the second-best defense in the league.

Before the 2003 season, they acquired running back Stephen Davis. Once Delhomme replaced Rodney Peete at halftime of the opener, the team took flight, eventually finishing 11–5. The Panthers beat Dallas in their Wild Card game for the honor of traveling to face St. Louis. Up 11 points with three minutes left, they let Kurt Warner's Rams score a touchdown and a two-point conversion, recover an onside kick, and add a field goal to tie the score. After a scoreless first overtime, Delhomme hit Steve Smith on a 69-yarder for the win in what remains the most exciting moment in team history. The Panthers then beat Philadelphia and met New England in Super Bowl XXXVIII. They trailed 14–10 through three periods before the teams combined for 37 fourth-quarter points, including a Super Bowl-record 85-yard scoring pass from Delhomme to Muhammad. The Panthers tied the game on a Ricky Proehl touchdown with 1:08 left, only to see the Patriots prevail 32–29 on a last-second field goal.

Following an injury-riddled 7–9 season in 2004, the team rode Smith, its best offensive weapon, to the 2005 NFC title game, falling 34–14 to Seattle. Then came 8–8 and 7–9 finishes, the latter year marked by Delhomme's bad elbow and 44-year-old Vinny Testaverde's final go-round. The 2008 season was noteworthy for the emergence of running back DeAngelo Williams but even more for the Panthers' unity after Smith punched out teammate Ken Lucas during the pre-season, the second such act by the tightly wound receiver.

More than the Carolinas' other pro teams, the Panthers seem here to stay. Though they fulfilled Richardson's promise of reaching the Super Bowl within 10 years, they have the look of a small-market franchise that musters a run at the ring every few years but otherwise resides in the middle of the pack.

Panthers fans may not like that assessment, but in the pithy words of the coach himself, it is what it is.

—Stephen Kirk

The Carolina Hurricanes

Come on already, people. The Hurricanes have been in North Carolina since 1997. The game is *hockey*, not *ice hockey*.

I was one of the lonely few who saw the team play in Greensboro during the two years between its departure from Connecticut and the completion of what is now the RBC Center in Raleigh. I remember hearing an interview with one of the 'Canes—either perennial All-Star Ron Francis or leading scorer Keith Primeau. What did it feel like, the reporter asked, to play in front of such a paltry home crowd?

Actually, the Greensboro Coliseum could seat 21,000 people, making it the largest arena in the National Hockey League. But attendance was such that officials curtained off most of the upper deck. The scene was embarrassing for a casual fan and must have been exponentially so for a major league athlete.

But the 'Canes player didn't take the bait. The Hurricanes were happy to be in North Carolina, he answered. They understood that most fans were making a 90-minute drive from the Triangle after putting in a full day at the office or factory, he said. They very much appreciated the people who showed up.

That reply is typical of the Hurricanes and the NHL in general. Perhaps because hockey runs a distant last place among the four major North American sports, the players seem to have an appreciation for their exalted status. Professional football players have a deserved reputation for toughness, but if you catch one of them in a post-game interview, he may look like he stepped off the set after filming a commercial with the Manning brothers. Watch an interview with a hockey player, however, and you'll see a man richly decorated with welts, like he just got caught stealing Gordie Howe's lunch. But you'll be surprised at his grace, well-spokenness, and sportsmanship. The word *gentleman* may come to mind.

The franchise was born in 1971 as the New England Whalers of the World Hockey Association. The team played in Boston until poor attendance forced a move to Hartford, Connecticut, in 1975. Such a loyal following developed that the Whalers were one of four teams welcomed into the NHL when the leagues merged in 1979. Renamed the Hartford Whalers, the team had only three winning seasons in nearly 20 years in what was the smallest American market in the NHL. When it came time for a new arena, owner Peter Karmanos moved the team to North Carolina, changed its colors from navy, green, and silver to red, black, white, and silver, and selected the Carolina Hurricanes name himself.

The lame-duck stay in Greensboro was judged necessary because the only hockey venue in Raleigh was Dorton Arena, an aging, undersized facility on the state fairgrounds. Good news arrived when the team made the playoffs its second season in Greensboro. Tragedy followed when defenseman Steve Chaisson died in a one-car drunk-driving wreck after a series loss to the Boston Bruins.

Once the Hurricanes moved to their long-term home in Raleigh, they attracted a sizable, loud, and increasingly knowledgeable fan base, against the predictions of many. Those "Caniacs" even brought a couple of new wrinkles to NHL fandom—college-football-style tailgating and crowds at the airport to welcome the team home from road trips.

The 'Canes achieved considerable—if not consistent—success on the ice, too. They made the 2001 playoffs but fell in six games to the powerful New Jersey Devils, the defending champions. Coach Paul Maurice led them farther the following season. They flipped the opening-round series on favored New Jersey this time, winning four games to two. The 'Canes then beat Montreal in the second round and Toronto in the conference finals. Their reward was a date with the Detroit Red Wings—the consensus best team in the league—in the Hartford/Carolina franchise's first-ever trip to the Stanley Cup finals. Expectations were low everywhere outside the Carolinas, yet the Hurricanes surprised the Red Wings in game one, winning in overtime on a Ron Francis goal. The series went according to form after that, Detroit sweeping the next four contests, though the Hurricanes did force a triple-overtime thriller in Raleigh in game three.

The team tanked the next two seasons, going 22–43–11 in 2002–3 and 28–34–14 in 2003–4. Paul Maurice was replaced by Peter Laviolette, soon to become the winningest American-born coach in NHL history. Laviolette had considerable time to retool the Hurricanes, as the 2004–5 season was cancelled by a lockout.

The 'Canes' dream season came in 2005–6. Led by versatile tough-guy captain Rod Brind'Amour—a.k.a. "Rod the Bod"—and rising star Eric Staal, they finished 52–22–8, tied for third best in the league. With the team down two games in its opening-round series against Montreal, rookie Cam Ward replaced Martin Gerber in goal, and the romp was on. The Hurricanes won the next four over Montreal, then beat New Jersey in five games, then took a bitter seven-game series against the Buffalo Sabres, scoring three goals in the final period of the deciding game, including the winner by Brind'Amour. Facing the Edmonton Oilers in the finals, the 'Canes took a 3–1 lead in games and looked to be headed to glory, only to nearly blow the Stanley Cup when the Oilers won the next two contests. But the Hurricanes regrouped for a 3–1 victory in game seven in front of a wild crowd in Raleigh. Their 2006 Stanley Cup remains the only major league championship for a Carolinas team in any sport.

After the team missed the playoffs in 2007 and 2008, Peter Laviolette was fired and Paul Maurice brought back as coach. Also returning was Ron Francis, hired as an associate coach. In many ways, "Ronnie Franchise" remains the face of the Hurricanes. Drafted by the club's Hartford incarnation, the Hall of Famer played 10 seasons with the Whalers before winning a pair of Stanley Cups with Pittsburgh. He signed with the Hurricanes as a free agent during their second season in Greensboro and played five more years. Though big, durable, and highly skilled, Francis was best known for being the smartest player on the ice. Think Greg Maddux in baseball. It will be a major surprise if Francis isn't good at his new job.

If you've never seen the Hurricanes live, you'd be well advised to sit in the cheap seats, as it's easier for a newcomer to follow the puck from on high. You'll be amazed at the speed of the action and the hell-bent-for-leather attitude of the players—this in a game whose championship honors a guy named Stanley and whose sportsmanship trophy is the Lady Byng.

—STEPHEN KIRK

3
THE PLAYERS

An Elegy for Ernie Shore

By Ed Southern

Few outside of Forsyth County, North Carolina, have heard of Ernie Shore.

So imagine this Forsyth County native's surprise when the announcers covering baseball at the 2008 Summer Olympics mentioned Shore, and told the story of his most notable baseball achievement. Imagine my shock and disgust when they got that story wrong.

Fewer and fewer inside Forsyth County know why they have heard of Ernie Shore, why his name is on the minor league field tucked between the Dixie Classic Fairgrounds and the Reynolds tobacco warehouses. Fewer and fewer can remember the man himself, his long and productive life, and fewer have heard this story:

On June 23, 1917, Babe Ruth—then a pitcher for the Boston Red Sox—started a game against the Washington Senators by walking the first batter. Ruth argued the call and got himself ejected. The manager sent in Shore. Babe Ruth and Ernie Shore had begun their pro careers together with the then-minor-league Baltimore Orioles; they were called up together by the Red Sox, and often roomed together on the road. Rumor had it that the 6-foot-4-inch, 220-pound Shore was the only man on the team who could handle Ruth when the Babe lost his temper.

With very little warm-up, Shore came in for Ruth against the Senators. The lead-off man was picked off trying to steal second. Shore then retired each Senators batter in order, pitching only the third perfect game in modern major league history.

Of course, Shore's wasn't a perfectly perfect game. He was not the starting pitcher, and the first batter had reached first. Some baseball historians have called it a "perfect game in relief," which is a nonsensical phrase in the unyielding world of baseball statistics. Some have argued that Shore ought at least to get credit for a no-hitter.

The story, though, like the feat itself, is a great one, and deserving of remembrance no matter how it is recorded. NBC's Olympic broadcasters told it well: the lead-off walk, the argument and ejection, the 26 subsequent batters sent down in order. They only made one mistake in their re-telling: they switched the roles that Shore and Ruth played. They told their nationwide audience that Shore had walked the lead-off man, and that Ruth had pitched the imperfectly perfect game.

Such a switch has a certain logic to it. An imperfectly perfect game seems a Ruthian feat, as larger-than-life as calling his shot, hitting a World Series home run for a sick child, building Yankee Stadium. In the pop-

The Players

ular imagination, even in the imagination of baseball geeks, there's no such thing as a Shorian feat.

Ernie Shore was a good, but not quite a great, pitcher. He had a career win-loss record of 65–43, with a 2.47 Earned Run Average and 309 strikeouts. In 1915, he was 18–8 with a 1.64 ERA. In his two World Series (1915 and 1916), his record was 3–1. He missed the 1918 season while serving in the U.S. Navy; when he returned in 1919, the Sox sold him to the Yankees, blazing the trail that Ruth would soon follow. (Was the Curse of the Bambino really the Curse of Ernie Shore?) An arm injury sustained late in the 1917 season, and aggravated during his Navy service, took away much of Shore's velocity, though. He retired from baseball in 1922, just as his old roommate, now moved to the outfield, was becoming the Sultan of Swat.

"There are no second acts in American lives," F. Scott Fitzgerald said, famously and foolishly. American lives are all about second acts; America, for most if not all practical purposes, was founded for second acts. Ernie Shore left New York and came to Winston-Salem, North Carolina, not far from his native East Bend. He married and began a family. He sold cars until the Depression, then tried to make a living selling insurance. According to his 1980 obituary in the *Winston-Salem Journal*, by 1936 Shore was $20,000 in debt, trying to support a wife and three children, when he decided to run for sheriff of Forsyth County. He campaigned before and after working his day job. He won, and held the post for the next 34 years. He took over a sheriff's department with six men, and left it with 70 deputies. He got the department its first patrol cars, and later got the first two-way radios in the state for them. He aided the campaign to bring minor league baseball to Winston-Salem, and the new ball park built to house the team was and is named Ernie Shore Field in his honor. He was known for a gentle, almost humble, manner in his dealings as sheriff—not the most common words applied to Southern law enforcement in the mid-20th century. At Shore's death, *Winston-Salem Sentinel* columnist Tom Sieg wrote, "Ernie Shore's friends and contemporaries were saying the same things about him today that they said while he was alive—he was a great guy, a true gentleman and a good person to be around."

As a ballplayer, Ernie Shore deserves to have the story of his imperfectly perfect game told right. NBC got the story wrong and denied Shore the proper credit. Soon Winston-Salem's minor league team will move into a brand-new stadium near downtown, leaving Ernie Shore Field to Wake Forest's college team, and one more remembrance of Shore the ballplayer will be lost.

As an ex-ballplayer, though, Shore earned the respect and affection of family, friends, and a whole county of constituents. That's more to his credit than that one walked batter would have been, and it really makes no difference how many or how few remember it.

"Shoeless" Joe Jackson

"Shoeless" Joe Jackson's final resting place is not in an Iowa *Field of Dreams*, but in Greenville, South Carolina. I've seen his grave.

So much of Jackson's life, though, is shrouded in mysteries—in unanswered questions, legends, rumors, maybes—that if a movie about baseball's ghosts and myths is going to center on any one ballplayer, it almost has to be Shoeless Joe.

Born in an Upstate South Carolina mill town in 1887, Jackson barely went to school before starting work alongside his father in the textile mill. He was playing for the mill's baseball team by the time he was 13, and semi-pro ball by the time he was 18. He quickly made the minor leagues with the Philadelphia Athletics' farm system, and soon was bouncing between the minors and the majors. Traded to the Cleveland Naps (later the Indians), he played his first full major league season in 1911.

Of all America's major sports, baseball is our purest and therefore most merciless game of numbers: wins and losses, starts and saves, batting average, on-base percentage. Three strikes and you're out.

Purely on the numbers, Shoeless Joe is one of the greatest ballplayers ever. He hit .408 in his rookie season, still the highest rookie batting average ever. His batting average was above .340 for eight of his thirteen major league seasons. He finished his career with 1772 hits and 785 Runs Batted In. His career .356 batting average is third-best in major league history.

If you factor in the legends, the rumors, the maybes, Jackson becomes not just a great ballplayer but the stuff of which folk heroes are made. He started his pro career as a pitcher, but threw the ball so hard that he broke his catcher's arm, and was moved to the outfield. He had a swing so pure that Babe Ruth admitted copying it. He earned the nickname "Shoeless" when he played a game in his stocking feet, after a new pair of shoes had given him blisters the day before.

And then there's the big maybe of Jackson's career and life, the one that turned him from a folk hero into a tragic hero: Did Shoeless Joe conspire with gamblers and White Sox teammates to throw the 1919 World Series, the one forever known as "the Black Sox series"? Jackson admitted in court to agreeing to take the gamblers' money, but those merciless numbers show that Jackson also hit .375 in that series, with no errors. A grand jury acquitted him, but Judge Kennesaw Mountain Landis, the first commissioner of Major League Baseball, banned Jackson for life—and, as it turned out, beyond, as Jackson remains ineligible to enter the Baseball Hall of Fame.

There are things in baseball more merciless than its numbers.

After the ban, Jackson played for and managed several minor league and semi-pro teams in South Carolina and Georgia. He and his wife Katie opened a dry-cleaners in Savannah, Georgia, and later a liquor store in Greenville. (Leading to yet another legend: once, they say, Ty Cobb came into Jackson's store, but Jackson showed no sign of knowing him. Finally Cobb asked, "Don't you know me, Joe?" Jackson told Cobb that of course he knew him, but "wasn't sure you wanted to know me.") Jackson died and was buried in Greenville in 1951.

Jackson always proclaimed his innocence of the fix. Later evidence seemed to give credence to Jackson's stand: his teammates admitted that Jackson was never at their meetings with the gamblers; the White Sox attorney forced Jackson to sign a waiver of immunity that Jackson, who was practically if not totally illiterate, couldn't even read. The films *Eight Men Out* and, of course, *Field of Dreams*, based on the W. P. Kinsella novel *Shoeless Joe*, brought Shoeless Joe and the Black Sox back into the public eye and cast them in a sympathetic light. In 1999, the United States House of Representatives passed a motion honoring Jackson's career and asking MLB to rescind his ban (MLB has not, as of this writing). Greenville has honored him by moving his house to the West End, next to the town's new minor league stadium, and turning it into the Shoeless Joe Jackson Museum and Baseball Library.

"Jackson's fall from grace is one of the real tragedies of baseball," Connie Mack, hardly a softie, once said. "I always thought he was more sinned against than sinning."

It seems, though, that Jackson's tragedy, while keeping him out of the Hall of Fame, has brought him more fame than almost any other player of his era.

—Ed Southern

Choo Choo

By Ron Green, Sr.

Charlie "Choo Choo" Justice, who defined the word "hero" for a generation, is dead.

Roughly half a century has passed since Justice was running, passing and kicking North Carolina's Tar Heels into two Sugar Bowls and a Cotton Bowl and capturing the imagination of a nation that literally sang his praises. Many of you won't even recognize the name, but take the word of those of us who have lived long: We have lost the most heroic figure ever to play a sport in this state.

Not the greatest athlete, but the athlete around whom glory wrapped itself most lovingly.

Others have come along and broken his records. In basketball, Michael Jordan made Justice's accolades pale by comparison.

The games have changed, become more sophisticated. Athletes are bigger and faster and more specialized. Commerce has elbowed its way deep into collegiate sports.

There is a harder edge to it all now. Our eyes are no longer wide in awe, but narrowed in scrutiny. We have changed and there can never be another Choo Choo Justice, because there will never be another era, another time of wonder, like that in which he played.

A Time for Heroes

Justice would have been a star in any time, but he came back from Coast Guard duty to Chapel Hill when the nation was ready to turn its attention to the playing fields and away from World War II, which had only recently ended. It was the late 1940s. People were singing love songs. Television had not yet replaced imagination. Money didn't dominate the sports pages.

People gave freely of their adoration, a trait they had learned in wartime. There was a wonderful innocence, an innocence that would soon be lost.

There could not have been a more romantic time to be a triple-threat tailback on a powerful college football team.

And along came this unimposing figure, this 170-pounder from Asheville, his head tilted to one side out of habit, his features handsome, his name—Justice—engaging and his nickname—Choo Choo—perfect. With a football in his hand, he was like the wind, speeding, slowing, changing direction. "Swivelhipped" is how it was described back then. He had a natural talent, of course, but he had practiced it by running the hills in downtown Asheville, darting in and out of foot traffic during the Christmas shopping season.

Originally published in the Charlotte Observer, *October 2003.*

Making make-believe tacklers miss. Running to daylight. Running to glory.

'A Bad Heart'? Not Quite

Justice was born May 18, 1924.

He missed the first two years of grammar school because of anemia and later was advised not to play football or any other strenuous sport because, he was told by a doctor, he had "a bad heart." By the time he was 15, though, Justice was in a junior high school uniform, weighing all of 125 pounds. The next year, he was a second-string tailback in high school. The following year, he moved up to first string and led Asheville High to an 11–0 record and then, as a senior, to a 9–0 mark. For his high school career, he gained 4,005 yards rushing in 286 carries, completed 41 of 66 passes, averaged 40.5 yards for 50 punts and scored 49 touchdowns, averaging 34.4 yards per score. And he generally played less than three quarters.

He was equally dazzling in Coast Guard football and was heavily recruited by college coaches. He had decided to go to South Carolina, but his brother talked him into staying in the state, and he chose North Carolina over Duke.

On a powerful Tar Heels team that featured a wealth of service veterans, Justice wove a legend that today has an ethereal quality to it, like ghost stories told in the mountains around his hometown.

When he was out there, anything seemed possible to the packed houses that came to see him play. You knew, sooner or later, he would do something to bring you to your feet screaming.

Against Tennessee, he ran 74 yards from scrimmage for one touchdown. Thirteen times the Volunteers had their hands on him and couldn't hold him.

Against Florida, he had a 75-yard touchdown run and a 90-yard kickoff return for a score. Against Texas, on one possession, he returned a punt 39 yards, ran for 21 and then passed to fellow All-American Art Weiner for the touchdown.

Against Georgia, he returned a punt 94 yards to score. Against Virginia, he had an 80-yard TD run. Against Oklahoma in the Sugar Bowl, he ran for 9, 10, 13, 25, 11, 14 and 8 yards and punted for 65, 65, 57 and 53 yards.

And so it went for four seasons, and Justice became everybody's idol, and everybody's All-American, but he remained painfully modest, and that never changed, ever. He could have won two Heisman Trophies and should have won one, but Doak Walker, another great runner, beat him out for one, and Leon Hart, a Notre Dame end, was a surprise winner of the other.

A song was written about Justice, "All The Way, Choo Choo," that got national play. A book, *Choo Choo: The Charlie Justice Story*, was written about him. A sermon was preached about him in a Baptist church. The Christian Athletes Foundation honored him in 1949 for "courage in the face of terrific physical punishment and unexpected defeat, for humility in the face of many honors, for loyalty to the church and for giving of time and interest to unfortunate children, for clean living and good sportsmanship in general."

Didn't Need the NFL

Justice tried the NFL with the Washington Redskins and in one game ran 11 times for 199 yards, but he soon abandoned the pro game. His size worked against him and he played with a team that was struggling. He never said it, but he might have quit to preserve what had come before, to assure that he didn't leave the game with bad memories. Sundays in Washington were a million miles from Saturdays in Chapel Hill. From the start, he had not wanted to play pro ball, so leaving it was easy.

Long after he had settled into private life with an insurance company, Justice was often asked to make public appearances.

A woman from eastern North Carolina called me one day to ask how to contact Choo Choo.

She wanted to invite him to speak to some group. She said she couldn't pay him anything.

I relayed the message to him and he contacted her and went and spoke. For free.

"I'm not worried about being paid," he said. "I'm just pleased that they still remember me."

Junior Johnson

Saying Junior Johnson was just a stock car driver is like saying Daniel Boone was just a hunter.

Junior Johnson was not the first NASCAR driver. He may not have even been the best. But he set the standard, not so much for what a NASCAR driver is supposed to do (drive fast, turn left, and win races), but for what a NASCAR driver is supposed to be.

Like Daniel Boone, he had something about him that inspired fascination, respect, even awe. His reputation brought Tom Wolfe—white suit, spats, and all—to Wilkes County, North Carolina, and inspired the writer to call Johnson "the last American hero" in the pages of *Esquire*. He is, to my knowledge, the only NASCAR driver and North Carolinian ever name-checked in song by Bruce Springsteen (in "Cadillac Ranch"). More than any other driver, he fully embodied NASCAR's history and foundation myths; more than any other driver or owner, he pointed NASCAR toward its future.

Robert Glenn Johnson, Jr., was born in 1931 in Wilkes County. He grew up helping in the two family businesses: farming and moonshining. He was behind a mule, plowing a field, when he was invited to drive in his first professional race. He left the plow, put on his shoes, and went straight to the North Wilkesboro Speedway; he finished second.

Since age 14 he had been running loads of illegal liquor through the North Carolina mountains, and was never caught behind the wheel of a car. He was caught, however, tending the family still, and spent 11 months in a federal penitentiary. Before his arrest he was already a racer of note, having won five races and finished sixth in the points standings in his first full NASCAR season, the year before his arrest, and had intended to retire from moonshining to race full-time. After his release, he was hell on wheels.

Driving without the support of a manufacturer (meaning he built and modified all his cars himself), Johnson won 50 races in NASCAR's Grand National circuit, the precursor to the current Sprint Cup series. He also won 46 poles, and had 148 top 10 finishes in 313 races.

Along the way, he invented the technique of drafting (putting your car into the slipstream of the car ahead, then sling-shotting around to take the lead), now a standard tactic in motorsports. He was the first driver to use a two-way radio to communicate with his crew chief—and was also the first driver to turn off the radio to better ignore his crew chief's instructions.

He retired from driving in 1966 and became a car owner, fielding his own NASCAR team. As owner, he won six Winston Cup championships, three with Cale Yarborough, and three with Darrell Waltrip. More importantly for NASCAR,

Junior Johnson was responsible for the Winston Cup coming to be.

In the early 1970s, NASCAR faced a serious withdrawal of sponsor and manufacturer support, to the point that some teams would not be able to field cars for the 1971 season unless new sponsorship was found. Johnson realized that a recent ban on television advertising of cigarettes would leave tobacco companies with extra cash in their marketing budgets. He made the short drive from Wilkes County down Highway 421 to Winston-Salem, home of the R. J. Reynolds Tobacco Company, and met with Reynolds's Ralph Seagrave to discuss RJR's sponsorship of Johnson's team and, maybe, all of NASCAR. The end result was the renaming of the Grand National circuit as the Winston Cup series, with RJR putting up the prize money for the driver with the most Cup points at the end of each season. The infusion of cash revitalized NASCAR and revolutionized thinking about sponsorships and marketing, starting NASCAR on the path from regional to national sport.

Johnson no longer owns a NASCAR team, concentrating on smaller business ventures, including a co-ownership in Piedmont Distillers, North Carolina's only legal distiller. In 1986, President Ronald Reagan gave Johnson a full pardon for his 1956 moonshining conviction. He was named one of NASCAR's 50 Greatest Drivers during NASCAR's 50th anniversary celebrations in 1998, and is an inductee in both the International and National Motorsports Halls of Fame. From the Wilkes County line to the Windy Gap exit, U.S. Highway 421, where Johnson once outran the revenuers, is now officially known as the Junior Johnson Highway.

—Ed Southern

Synchronized Swim

By Betty Brown

"If anyone from my Red Hat Club mentions my being on the synchronized swim team in the 1956 Olympics, just play along," Mrs. Opal Pickles says to her comic strip husband after attending a meeting where she discovers others in her club were beauty queens and NASCAR drivers in their earlier years.

Actually, I really was on the Dolphins synchronized swimming team at Queens College in the mid-'50s. Most of the time, I was assigned to perform out of the water, on the deck that surrounded the pool. Those of us who had that awesome task were choreographed to simulate ice skaters to "The Skaters' Waltz" while the more proficient ladies did tricks in and under the water.

You see, I have what I consider a handicap, having to wear nose plugs. There is something about being upside down in a swimming pool that makes a valve between my nose and throat shut down its true function of keeping chlorine water out of my lungs. I have had this deformity all my life, but have learned that a good set of plugs avoids the drowning process that tends to take over during a performance, where back flips and surface dives are considered essential. This necessity of wearing nose plugs did take away, a little, from the grace and swan-like beauty of the routines.

I'm not sure that being assigned to the pool deck helped matters, as I often reflect on synchronized swimmers looking rather odd wearing nose plugs on dry land.

Our uniform swimsuits at Queens were handed out with a towel upon entering the pool area of the gym. We were bestowed with cotton knit suits, color-coded according to size. If you saw the suits, you would immediately be cognizant of the fact that the suits were not designed by Jantzen or Cole of California. Most of the average-size ladies wore royal blue; there were a few petites in pink, and another group in slate blue who were a bit above average. Then there were three or four of us who had to go to mint green, including one short but very overweight sophomore, and myself. (Peanut butter and jelly were staples on each table in the dining room of Morrison Hall.) I could get into the slate blue suit, but my torso, rather on the long side, tended to encourage aggravating wedgie-like symptoms. The mint green suit didn't ride up as much. But wearing the mint green remained a little awkward amidst the majority of royal blue Queenies. They didn't have Oprah in those days to tell them that the long torsos would look better in royal blue, which is darker and avoids taking on the look of an oversized after-dinner mint.

In my seventies now, I have developed what my gerontologist refers to as a postnasal drip. I have begun to combat that ailment by using "Simply Saline," an over-the-drug-store-counter product. The container sports a pump capable of great blasts of a saline solution forced into sinuses and supposedly prevents professional figure skater Sasha Cohen from catching colds. The instructions on the can advise leaning over the lavatory and pumping until the solution douses the sinus cavities and runs back out a nostril into the sink. This process takes me back to the '50s and the feeling of drowning that I experienced before I learned to depend on my nose plugs. So, I conjecture, spraying minimally in an upright position avoids being overcome with that drowning sensation I attribute to my faulty nasal valve.

The most valuable gain derived from this experience of ages past is to be able to show my granddaughters some moves to synchronize while floating and sculling around in Banks Channel at Wrightsville Beach. If only I had a decent pair of nose plugs, I could show them some really awesome tricks.

Arnold Palmer

Tiger Woods may be chasing Jack Nicklaus' record of 19 major championships, but he's living in a world that Arnold Palmer made.

Before Palmer came along, golf was a niche sport thought to be only for the well-born country club set. By the time Palmer retired, professional golf was watched by millions, including an entire army—Arnie's Army.

Palmer grew up in Latrobe, Pennsylvania, the son of the head professional and greenskeeper at Latrobe Country Club. He came south in 1947 to attend Wake Forest College on a golf scholarship, after his friend Bud Worsham, who already had a scholarship, talked the coach into giving Palmer one, too. Palmer, Worsham and the Deacon golf team won two conference championships before Worsham and another teammate were killed in an automobile accident. A distraught Palmer dropped out of Wake soon after and enlisted in the United States Coast Guard. Palmer returned to competitive golf after his three-year hitch was up, and his win in the 1954 U.S. Amateur Championship convinced him to try to make it on the PGA tour.

Sixty-two PGA wins, four Masters titles, two British Opens, and one U.S. Open later, Palmer can be said not only to have "made it" in professional golf, but to have made professional golf into the major sport it is today. In 1960, he was *Sports Illustrated*'s Sportsman of the Year; the Associated Press later named him the "Athlete of the Decade" for the 1960s. He was the first golfer to earn $1 million on the PGA Tour. He was the first client of Mark McCormack's IMG, which more or less invented the marketing of athletes as we know it. His common touch, affability and daring golf—not to mention his thrilling head-to-head battles with Nicklaus, Gary Player and other golfing greats—drew large television audiences to golf for the first time.

Years after his retirement from competitive golf, Palmer ranked near the top of endorsement earnings for athletes, proof of his widespread and persistent popularity.

—Ed Southern

Mary Garber Stood Very Tall in a Man's World

By Lenox Rawlings

The newspaper roster generously listed Mary Garber as 5 feet tall, yet she was the tallest person in almost every room.

Mary, who died yesterday at 92, towered over human prejudice and human smallness.

She wiggled free from the stereotypes and conventions and limitations of her time. She figured out ways to be her own person, to do what she wanted, to do a job she loved.

When the last male, a high-school student turning 18, left the *Twin City Sentinel*'s sports department and joined the Navy during World War II, Mary became the sports editor of the afternoon paper. She relinquished the role once the war ended and soldiers returned to their desks, including Sports Editor Carlton Byrd, but within a year Managing Editor Nady Cates acknowledged her natural instincts and reassigned her to sports.

For nearly 30 years, Mary was the only woman in the state on the sports beat full time. She will go down in history—big American history, not little local history—as a newspaper pioneer who represented the simple truth that everyone deserves a fair shot.

She lived that way. She treated others that way, just like her mother taught her. Race didn't matter. Religion didn't matter. Money didn't matter. Gender certainly didn't matter. She would warm up to folks if they acted right, and she would chide them if they behaved badly—although seldom to their faces and almost never without awarding a second or third chance to demonstrate a modicum of civility.

She lived among some of the richest old people in town without holding their wealth against them. She wrote stories about some of the poorest young people in town without holding their deficiencies against them. She made friends in every neighborhood and carried on grudges in none.

Unlike many public figures who proclaim themselves champions of civil rights, Mary didn't really see people as black or white or brown subdivisions. She saw them as individuals, capable of decency or deceit regardless of race.

After an avalanche of prominent awards and hall-of-fame inductions, Mary recalled her favorite tribute during an interview with Diane K. Gentry for an oral-history project sponsored by the Washington Press Club Foundation. The praise arrived by word of mouth from Mamie Braddy, a police reporter and friend who

Originally published in the Winston-Salem Journal, *September 2008.*

had lobbied editors to hire Mary. Mrs. Braddy, sitting in the stands at Bowman Gray Stadium during a soap-box derby, overheard a conversation between two black kids about 8 and 10 years old.

The older kid asked the younger one: "Do you see that lady down there on the field?"

"Yes."

"Do you know who she is?"

"No."

"That's Miss Mary Garber. And she don't care who you are or where you're from or what you are. If you do something, she's going to write about you."

The remark's innocent frankness appealed to Mary. "And," she said, "I'd like to have that on my tombstone."

She preferred candor. She would walk over and grin and mention a team I had covered the night before. "They aren't worth a flip, are they?" she'd say. Or maybe she'd use stronger language.

In reflective conversations, Mary brought up what she considered her shortcomings as a child football player tackling boys, as a writer tackling descriptive phrases, as a rookie news reporter covering a union drive and as *The Sentinel*'s society-page editor.

"I was definitely not cut out to be society editor," she said. "You'd have to write about women wearing red dresses with flowers. I didn't know diddle-do about that."

Faced with such a story, she recruited a friend who worked in the clothing section of a department store to interpret the fashions as the women paraded by.

Mary preferred pulling up her incurably floppy socks and putting on her tennis shoes. She pulled for the underdog. She often worked like a dog, not because someone ordered her but because that came with the territory.

As a young woman working in a man's world, she couldn't enter locker rooms and hear the original recollections of games just played. She couldn't join the social wing of the sportswriting fraternity until someone asked her, partly because her personal code and shy side precluded Mary from inviting herself.

On her first business trip to Duke, a university she once considered attending because she adored its formidable football team, Mary was denied access to the press box and relegated to a private box filled with chatty coaches' wives and restless children.

An editor at the paper wrote letters to the major North Carolina colleges, which promptly ended that separate-and-unequal sham in 1946. Once inside the press boxes, Mary sometimes suffered the indignity of coarse stage whispers from dim male reporters challenging her professional rights.

"Jackie Robinson was breaking in with the Dodgers about then," she said, citing her hero on the occasion of her official semi-retirement in 1986. "He had to take a lot of crap when he came up. His philosophy was: 'Do the best job you could and keep your mouth shut. People will eventually respect you.' In my case, eventually, people would say, 'She's all right.' That's all I really wanted."

The first time I saw Mary, I saw her cap first. It was a tennis cap, a dark model similar to a baseball cap but without the high crown. She wore the cap slightly cocked to one side and pulled down snugly, so that it nearly touched the top of her wire-rimmed glasses and blocked out distractions during the tennis match we were covering.

The second time I saw Mary, I saw her cap first again. It was a knitted wool cap, dark and dense and a bit askew. That seemed strange—indoors—but the circumstances were ten times stranger.

In the chaotic cubbyhole outside the basketball locker rooms at Duke, Mary perched her busy little body on an equipment trunk and waited. She bided her time outside the inner sanctums of male athletics that night, as she usually did back in 1971, and relied on sports-information aides to produce interview subjects. She did not wait patiently, fidgeting in her thick jacket and turning her head constantly.

Amid the swirl of activity—student managers hauling stacks of towels, reporters hurrying from one locker room to the other, parents and friends squeezing into the remaining square inches—Mary stood out, even though she was more or less sitting on one foot, the other dangling off the trunk's side.

Finally, a coach approached her, after he had finished talking to other reporters in the locker room. She started asking questions and scribbling down the answers with the blunt nub of a No. 2 pencil. (Over the years, I saw Mary sharpen a thousand pencils, but somehow I never managed to see her use one that had a sharp point.) Every now and then, she would peer over her glasses and curl her lips in her unique way, presaging yet another question.

At the time, as a college student covering the game for a Raleigh newspaper, I didn't think much about what the woman might have gone through to reach that jammed ACC passageway. I didn't even consider her wildly unusual, since about half the journalism students I knew were women, and quite a few reporters at the Raleigh *News & Observer*. Their equality was assumed—in concept, if not fact—but the issue of equal access obviously remained unresolved.

Mary helped resolve it.

Although way overdue, she got her due, including: the presidency of at least two sportswriting groups that had rejected her original applications; the Red Smith Award from Associated Press sports editors; membership in the N.C. Sports Hall of Fame and the U.S. Basketball Writers Association Hall of Fame. The *Winston-Salem Journal*, the ACC and the U.S. Tennis Association named annual awards for her.

She didn't foresee all this as a child, of course. Mary was born at home on Riverside Drive in New York, on April 19, 1916. Her father, Mason Garber, a civil engineer and partner in a family construction company, took on the job of building Winston-Salem's train station in 1924.

The Garbers encouraged their three daughters to keep grandparents informed about their new world. Mary's older sister, Helen, and her younger sister, formally Cornelia but better known as Neely, wrote letters. Mary deemed that quite dull. She made up a newspaper front page and plugged stories into different spots, with headlines. Thus began *Garber News*, which was the start of a newspaper career that seemed more inevitable as she worked on local school papers and her alma mater, Hollins University (class of 1938).

Mary's older sister became an accomplished pianist, and her younger sister a horseback rider and instructor. Mary became a sportswriter. She remained a *Journal* sportswriter for 16 years after her retirement, until her eyes and legs gave out, until she had to accept everyday medical care and leave Neely behind at the house.

Mary always gave Neely credit for handling chores that made the newspaper career possible, particularly after their mother became an invalid.

Neely died last fall. After the funeral and the graveside remarks at St. Paul's Episcopal Church, relatives and friends reassembled in a sunny church meeting room to honor Neely's request for a casual celebration.

People lined up to greet Mary, who sat in her wheelchair and carried on one short conversation after another, summoning strength I didn't know she had. Someone brought Mary a plate and a glass.

Folks stood in clusters around the room, talking and eating and drinking for quite a while. The weight of mourning felt lighter, and the memories of Neely felt brighter, and it seemed like the right time to leave.

Walking toward the doorway, I looked back and saw Mary turn her glass upside down and empty it dry. As she lowered the glass, near the end of the exhausting day, there was the hint of a smile.

Mary lived a full and useful life, right to the last drop.

David Thompson

Monte Towe, David Thompson, and Tommy Burleson. They made an interesting snapshot. Small, medium, and double extra-large.

At 5'7", Towe was big enough to be All ACC in basketball, to play college baseball, and to take the floor in the ABA and the NBA.

Burleson, the 7'4" "Newland Needle" from the North Carolina mountains, held his own against Bill Walton and assorted Olympic and NBA centers.

But on David Thompson's N.C. State team, they were like the two proverbial brunettes standing beside the blonde. They just weren't destined to be the center of attention.

Fans of freshman eligibility should thank Thompson. So should anyone who likes slam dunking in the college game. In many eyes, Thompson is the player who inspired those rule changes. Vertical-leap measurements were unknown before he came along. Thompson's is generally reported at 44 inches. He and Towe are said to have invented the alley-oop.

The son of a minister and one of 11 children, Thompson grew up in a shack on a dirt road in Shelby, west of Charlotte. When he chose N.C. State after starring at Crest High, he capped off two great recruiting years by Coach Norm Sloan—first Burleson, then Towe, 6'4" Thompson, and 6'7" Tim Stoddard. Like Towe, Stoddard played a little baseball, ultimately making 485 appearances as a relief pitcher in the majors.

State fans had to wait until Burleson was a junior and Thompson, Towe, and Stoddard were sophomores before their four blue-chippers took the floor together. Even worse, the Wolfpack was ineligible for the post-season that 1972–73 season, Thompson having played a pick-up game with assistant coach Eddie Biedenbach on a recruiting visit to Raleigh, a rules violation. As it turned out, that sanction denied State the chance at consecutive national titles.

Thompson was an immediate sensation, scoring 33 points and grabbing 13 rebounds his first varsity game. The Wolfpack finished the season a perfect, if frustrated, 27–0. Thompson averaged 24.7 points. And that was on a bad leg. He had torn knee cartilage repaired in the off-season and came back quicker and more confident his junior year.

The 1973–74 season began with an anomaly atop the national rankings—two teams that had completed the previous year undefeated. John Wooden's UCLA Bruins, the winners of seven consecutive NCAA titles, were number one. N.C. State was number two. Their matchup in St. Louis on December 15 was the most anticipated regular-season game since Houston beat UCLA in the

Astrodome in 1968. It didn't live up to its billing. UCLA's Ralph Drollinger caught Burleson with an elbow, breaking his nose and knocking out two teeth. State went down 84–66.

But that was the team's only loss. Game after game, the State players shed their prototypical '70s bell-bottom warmups and laid waste to the competition. They beat UNC twice by a combined four points, then beat them a third time by 11. They twice defeated a loaded Maryland team starring All-Americans Tom McMillen, Len Elmore, and John Lucas.

At the ACC Tournament in Greensboro, they defeated Virginia, then faced Maryland again. The Terrapins hit 12 of their first 14 shots. The Pack pulled to within five at halftime, then tied the game near the end of regulation, thanks to Burleson's 38 points. State won 103–100 in overtime in what some consider the greatest college game ever—and the one that paved the way to admitting more than one team per conference to the national tourney. Maryland lost despite shooting 61 percent. The teams combined for 203 points in an era without a shot clock, a three-point shot, or dunking. Maryland coach Lefty Driesell visited the State players after the game. "I'm proud of y'all," he said. He encouraged them to beat UCLA. They would soon have their chance.

First came NCAA Tournament dates with Providence and Pittsburgh at Reynolds Coliseum. The Pack went down by 12 early against a Pittsburgh team intent on roughing up Thompson. Usually careful about jumping in crowds, Thompson lost his cool in goaltending a shot, caught a foot on a teammate's shoulder, and crashed head-first to the court, where he lay unconscious in a pool of blood. Many in the crowd thought him dead. While Thompson was at the hospital, Walter Cronkite stayed on the phone with attendants to report on his condition. Meanwhile, Burleson and Stoddard got physical with Pittsburgh. By the time the heavily bandaged Thompson returned to the arena to thunderous applause, the Pack was on the way to a 100–72 victory behind Burleson's 35.

The Final Four was played in Greensboro. In the semi-finals, State and UCLA were tied at 35 at halftime, at 65 at the end of regulation, and at 67 after overtime. UCLA was up by seven in the second overtime when Towe took a charge, Burleson and Moe Rivers made steals, and Thompson scored late for an 80–77 State victory. The game's most memorable play was Thompson's lightning-quick block on Walton, still stunning to watch after 35 years. He scored 28 to Walton's 29.

The championship game was like the rest of Thompson's career—good but anticlimactic. State beat Marquette 76–64 for its first national title.

Following a loss in the ACC finals Thompson's senior year, N.C. State turned down an invitation to the NIT. "The NIT is for losers," Thompson remarked. Subsequently, the number-one pick in both the NBA and ABA drafts—by the Atlanta Hawks and the Virginia Squires, respectively—he ended up signing with the ABA's Denver Nuggets. His reason for choosing the lesser league? On his visit with the Hawks, he was treated to McDonald's.

During Thompson's rookie year, he and Julius Erving were the showcase performers in the first-ever slam dunk contest. Erving won. The next season, the Nuggets were absorbed into the NBA when the leagues merged. Thompson remained an outstanding scorer, averaging 25 points over his first six years with Denver. But he wasn't quite outstanding enough to carry a team on the pro level. His high point came in 1978. Trailing George Gervin slightly in the race to be the league's top scorer, Thompson put up 73 points in the season finale, only to see Gervin score 63 and win the title.

The pressure of being the highest-paid player in team sports got to Thompson. He missed practices and descended into cocaine and alcohol abuse. Near the end, while playing for Seattle, he fell down the steps while partying at Studio 54 in New York and severely damaged his knee. He retired in 1984 at age 30.

Though his road hasn't been easy, Thompson has worked to pull his life together. He lives in Charlotte, where he helps run a sports ministry that operates youth basketball leagues. Among the program's alumni is Stephen Curry, who went on to stardom at Davidson.

Now in his mid-50s, Thompson says he can still dunk. Those who disbelieve it never saw him play.

—STEPHEN KIRK

The World's Number One, Flat-Out, All-Time Great Driver: Richard Petty

From *The World's Number One, Flat-Out, All-Time Great Stock Car Racing Book*

By Jerry Bledsoe

The community of Level Cross lies on the edge of the North Carolina Piedmont, a crossroads on U.S. Highway 220, twelve miles south of Greensboro, five miles north of a little river-town called Randleman. There isn't much in Level Cross—neat, comfortable, middle-class houses, a trailer park, a couple of churches, a nice brick community center with a lighted baseball field out back, the new volunteer fire department building across the road—but it may be the best-known crossroads community in the South. The reason is Level Cross' only industry, No. 1 tourist attraction, and leading family. All bear the name Petty.

Stock car racing people do a lot of arguing about who is, or was, the greatest stock car racing driver of all time. Some say Fireball Roberts, some Curtis Turner, some David Pearson, and so on. But if the criteria for judging are to be the number of races and amount of money won, then the question is settled: Richard Petty is the greatest. He is so far out front that no other driver is ever likely to equal his record. He is *the* superstar of stock car racing.

Richard Petty lives less than a mile down the road from the volunteer fire station in a modest, red brick "ranch style" house. His younger brother, Maurice, one of racing's best mechanics, lives in another brick house across the road. Next door is a stately white house with a big front porch and a stone foundation, a house that Richard Petty's grandfather built. Here, with his wife Elizabeth, lives Lee Petty, now the family patriarch, a man who decided to go racing in the late forties and took his two young sons with him. Lee Petty became one of the great drivers of his day and held the record for winning races and national championships until his son came along and blitzed it. Next to the big white house, built around an old farmstead where Lee Petty put together his first race cars, is the center of Petty Enterprises, a cyclone-fence-enclosed compound of big blue-and-white steel buildings—a factory, no less, and the only product is race cars.

The Pettys were country people, simple, decent, God-fearing, and friendly, as most country people are, and they had remained country people. Perhaps as much as any other family, the Pettys represented what America was supposed to be about. They had believed and worked hard, and all the good things that were supposed to happen as a result had come to them. Yet it hadn't changed them. They were still the same down-to-earth people they had always been.

If any of the Pettys were going to change, it should have been Richard, for all the pressures and opportunities had surely been his. He had become rich and famous, a hero. He had paid his respects at the White House and toured Vietnam to visit the troops. Hollywood had made a movie about his life, and he had played the leading role (doing a credible job, too; he was at least as good an actor as, say, Elvis, or Rory Calhoun, both of whom had starred in dreadful stock car racing flicks). But his friends, neighbors, and the people around the racetracks would be the first to say that Richard Petty had never gotten "the big head."

"Same ol' Richard," says Ronnie Hucks, who has been a friend since high school days.

Richard sums up the Petty attitude succinctly: "A man don't want to git above his raisin's, you know."

Those "raisings" were humble indeed. One of Richard Petty's earliest and most vivid memories came at the age of six, in 1943, when his mother splashed some kerosene into the wood cooking stove one morning and it exploded, burning down the small frame Petty home before she had time to get anything out except herself and her two sons. The family moved into Richard's grandfather's house, where they stayed until the war ended, when Lee Petty built a tiny three-room house out of a construction trailer. He was doing a little farming then, growing tobacco and trying to make a go out of a little trucking business (some say that Lee Petty and his brother, Julie, also did a little likker hauling, although the Pettys do not acknowledge this). But a great deal of his time was spent breaking down cars and putting them back together with brother Julie. The front-yard was always strewn with old cars and car parts. Lee Petty had been obsessed with cars since he was 16 and gotten his first Model T. Nights he and Julie raced their cars on the red dirt roads around Level Cross. Guys with hot cars would come from as far away as Atlanta to race against the Petty brothers, and oftentimes there would be big money bet on those races. Some people around Level Cross would see Lee Petty speeding by, throwing up big clouds of red dust, and they would shake their heads and say that he was sure to come to no good—if he didn't get himself killed first.

By 1947, organized stock car races of a sort were being held at the Greensboro Fairgrounds and at a little track near Martinsville, Virginia, and the Petty brothers went to almost all of them. They were confident that they could put together a better car and drive it faster than anybody they saw at those races, and they began making plans to do just that. They bought a '39 Plymouth coupe and put a straight-eight Chrysler engine in it. By the time they'd finished rebuilding and refining it, they'd sunk nearly $4,000 into the project. It would take a lot of races to get that much money back, and the car would likely be torn up before they did it. Lee Petty made his formal racing debut in that car in 1948, however, and he was astounded when he finished only second. He had expected to completely dazzle the competition.

The following spring, the recently organized NASCAR announced plans for its first "new car" race at Charlotte, and Lee Petty was itching to get into it. He talked a friend into letting him borrow his '48 Buick Roadmaster for the race. He had raced the car on the back roads before and knew it would really run. He spent days preparing the car, and when the day of the race came, he loaded his family into it and drove off to Charlotte. The car gave him all the power he needed.

He was about to take the lead in the race when a sway bar broke and the Buick rolled four times. It took two wreckers to haul it off. The family had to hitch a ride back home, and Lee Petty had a lot of explaining to do to his friend, but that wreck had convinced him of one thing. He was going to have to get a lighter car.

By the time the first race was held at Darlington in 1950, Lee Petty had his light car. A Plymouth. Thus began an association between Plymouth and Petty that was to last for years, with only brief interruptions. At Darlington that day, the heavier cars began falling out under the pressure of the mounting mileage, but Lee Petty and Johnny Mantz, who was also driving a Plymouth, kept plugging away, always staying at the front, with Mantz finally beating out Petty to win.

But Lee Petty took second place in the point standings that year in his Plymouth, third the next and in 1954 he finally won his first championship. Two more would follow.

Richard was twelve and Maurice ten when their father started racing full time in 1950, and they both fancied themselves as racing mechanics. They went to all the races, and although there was a rule prohibiting anybody under eighteen from the pits, they usually managed to sneak around it. Their summers were hectic and exciting times, traveling to tracks around the South and in the North and Midwest, racing several times a week. They found themselves heroes to their classmates when they had to return to school in the fall, not so much because of the racing as for the traveling they had done.

High school had held no real interest for Richard except for athletics. He was 6-feet-2 and weighed over 180 pounds and he played football, basketball, and baseball for Randleman High, while managing to maintain a grade average close to B. Nights, he hurried home to help his father work on his car. He and Maurice had begun to learn the mechanics of a car when they first started traveling with their father. He let them do simple things at first, advanced them as they were ready. By the time he was eighteen, Richard was already building engines.

Lee Petty lived by maxims: Anything worth doing was worth doing well, he taught his sons. He also taught them that the person who works the longest, tries the hardest, always put forward the extra effort, is the one who wins. Richard and Maurice listened to his advice and saw the results.

When he was 21, Richard decided he would like to try his hand at driving in a race. He'd expressed some interest earlier, but his father asked him to wait until he was 21. It wasn't something that Richard had a burning passion to do. It was something he thought he ought to try, just to see if he liked it. He liked being a racing mechanic, and was sure that he would be happy making that his life's work, although he had once given some thought to going to college and becoming a high school coach, which was what his wife had hoped he would do.

"I never set out to be no superstar or nothing like that," he told me one night. "It was just something that happened over a long period of time. It was a gradual thing. One thing just builds on another, and I never had much time to think about it."

He and his cousin Dale Inman got ready an old Oldsmobile convertible that had been sitting near the house, and they took it off to Columbia, South Carolina, for Richard's first race. Lee Petty didn't go. He had another race that night. Lee Petty knew that there was no way to tell his son how to drive a race car. It was something that he would have to learn for himself. His only advice was: "Never drive a car faster than it feels good to you." Richard remembers that he was not at all nervous before that race. Driving a race car with other cars banging against it seemed to him a perfectly natural thing to be doing. He finished sixth that night, but he wouldn't have that good a finish again for a long time. He entered nine races his first year, tore up a lot of equipment, and won only $760, not a particularly impressive start.

Lee Petty had known that it would probably be like this, and he was not critical.

"After every race," Richard recalls, "he would set us down and say, 'Now, what did you learn from this race?'"

He was learning, and the next year, 1959, proved to be a good one for the Pettys. The new speedway at Daytona was opened that year, and Lee Petty won the first race there, although it was so close—three cars streaking across the line side by side—that it took the officials three days of studying photographs to decide who had won it. He went on to win an unprecedented third national championship for the year. Richard ran twenty-one races that year, racing against his father in most of them, but he says that there was never a father-son rivalry. He managed to finish six races in the top five that year, enough to bring home almost $8,000, although still not enough to turn a profit. He was showing promise, however, and NASCAR named him its first Rookie of the Year.

In July of that year, Richard had slipped off to Chesterfield, South Carolina, with a cute cheerleader from Randleman High School named Lynda Owens, and they were married by a justice of the peace. They had been going together for three years, having met while Maurice was dating a friend of Lynda's and they hoped to keep the marriage a secret, because Lynda still had a year of high school to finish. The secret was soon out, and they moved in with Richard's parents until they got themselves a trailer and parked it next door. Their first child, Kyle, was born the following year.

Richard won his first race in 1960, the year his son was born. That was at Charlotte. He thought he'd won the year before at Atlanta. He had taken the checkered flag, but another driver had kept on charging around the track and later demanded a recheck, claiming that there had been a scoring error.

"You didn't win," he told Richard. "*I* did."

The protesting driver, Lee Petty, was found to be correct and was declared the winner.

"I want the boy to win," Lee Petty told a reporter, "but I want him to *really* win. He didn't, so he doesn't deserve it."

There were three Pettys on the track during some races in 1960. Maurice had begun to drive, but his eyes were bad, and after he destroyed a car at Columbia, he quit and went back to building engines, at which he turned out to be a whiz. Richard came into his own as a driver that year, winning three races and more than $35,000, finishing second in the national championship.

He had little time to enjoy his success. Racing has its own way of humbling men, and it went to work on the Pettys early in 1961. They arrived at Daytona that year with two new Plymouths. Richard found himself starting in the first of the twin hundred-mile qualifying races. His father was to run in the second. On the last lap of the first race, Junior Johnson ran over something on the track and lost control. He hit Richard's car, sending it high up on the track—and over the wall, crashing into the parking lot far below.

For a moment, Richard sat stunned in the broken car. Then he crawled out through the empty space where the windshield had been and fell to the ground, spraining his ankle as he fell. He sat on the ground looking at the remains of his car until he realized that the engine was still running. He had crawled over to shut off the engine when the ambulance arrived.

At the track dispensary, the doctors found nothing seriously wrong. He was bruised and his ankle was painful, but he hobbled back to the pits, where his father was getting ready to start the second race. Just before the race began, Richard was suddenly struck by severe pain in his eyes. He was taken back to the dispensary, where the doctors discovered that his eyes were filled with tiny slivers of glass from the shattered windshield.

It took the doctors quite a while to get all of the glass out, and when Richard finally left the hospital, the race was almost finished. In the last lap, Banjo Matthews suddenly got sideways going into the first turn. Lee Petty, close behind, also started sliding, Johnny Beauchamp hit Lee Petty squarely in the side—T-boned him, in racing parlance—and froze with his foot full on the accelerator. Both cars went over the fence at the top of the bank and took flight. Richard started running toward the wreck, falling and stumbling because of his ankle. When he got to the wreckage, breathless and in pain, his father was being loaded into an ambulance. Richard had never seen race cars so badly damaged. His father was unconscious on the stretcher, limp and bleeding profusely. Richard climbed into a second ambulance and followed his father to the dispensary. There was a trail of blood leading inside when he got there, and the doctors were working hurriedly to stop the bleeding.

Lee Petty lingered near death for several days. He had been severely cut and bruised, a lung was punctured, and one leg was so badly smashed that the doctors feared that if he did live, he'd never be able to walk again without braces. When Lee Petty finally did regain consciousness for the first time, he looked up and saw Richard and told him to go on home, get another car ready to race, and he'd be on in a few days.

But Lee Petty remained hospitalized for four months. And Richard, 23, and Maurice, at 21, were left to run the family racing business by themselves. Neither of them knew anything about the business end of it, their father had always handled that, although Richard luckily had attended business college for several months after high school. They began to learn quickly, however. They got another car ready, and Richard ran all forty-two races on the circuit that year, bringing in $22,000, not a profitable season by a long shot, but it kept the Petty racing business alive.

By the 1962 season, Lee Petty was fully recovered. He walked with a slight limp, but he didn't need braces. He drove in a couple of races that season, but the spirit was no longer in him. It wasn't fun any more, he said, and he quit, leaving the responsibility of the family fortunes to Richard—who responded by winning eight races that year and eleven the next for more than a $100,000 in purses. In 1964, he won $99,000 and his first national championship.

Except for brief flings with Oldsmobiles, Chryslers, and Dodges, the Pettys had driven Plymouths exclusively. Lee Petty had made No. 42 famous. There was no special significance to the number. A sign painter had simply taken it from a license plate. Richard had followed by using No. 43, and he also painted all of his cars a certain brilliant blue that came to be known as "Petty blue." The color had no special significance either. It was the result of mixing a can of blue paint with a can of white because there wasn't enough of either to paint his car. But the color became one of the most popular on Plymouths sold in the South. When the car manufacturers were in racing, the Pettys were the Chrysler Corporation's No. 1 team. The manufacturers had come back into racing in 1963, and in 1965, when Chrysler pulled its drivers out to protest NASCAR's ban on its hemi engine, Richard and Maurice built a Barracuda, named it "Outlawed," numbered it "43 Jr.," and went drag racing.

At a dragstrip in Dallas, Georgia, something broke, Richard lost control, and the car careened up an embankment and hurtled into the crowd. Petty crawled from the car and sat, dazed, on the ground. A man came over angrily screaming, "You've killed a boy!" The boy was eight years old. Several other people were hurt. Petty, whose own son was five at the time, quit drag racing after that. That accident, he now says, is his only regret in all of his years of racing.

Chrysler and Petty returned to stock car racing in 1966. Petty won eight races that year, finished 20 out of 39 in the top five, and won $79,000. The next year was to be a record-setter. Everything seemed to fall into place, and Petty won 27 of the 48 races that year, 10 of them in a row, an unbelievable feat. That brought him $130,000 in purses and his second national championship. It took him three years to win that much money again, and it was not only unlikely, but almost impossible that anybody would ever win that many races in a season again.

But in 1971 he came close, winning 21 of 46 races and nearly $310,000 in purses, more money than any driver has ever won in a single year. That was the year that Chrysler finally pulled out of racing again, the last of the car manufacturers to do so. Petty quickly worked a deal with Andy Granatelli to have his STP Corporation sponsor the Petty Plymouth (later Dodge). *Time* reported that STP was funneling as much as $500,000 annually to Petty. "It might be that over a couple of years," says Petty, who, like most drivers, doesn't particularly care to discuss his financial affairs.

Richard Petty's third national championship came in 1971; his fourth, breaking his father's record, came the following year, when his winnings came to $227,000. By midseason of 1974, Petty had won 158 races (including five Daytona 500s) and more than $1,700,000 in purses in his career. His nearest competitor, David Pearson, had won 77 races.

Unlike some of the other good stock car drivers who have gone on to attempt other forms of racing, particularly in championship cars at Indianapolis, Petty, except for his brief stint in drag racing, has never ventured outside stock car racing. For that reason, racing experts have been reluctant to classify him as an all-around great race driver. That doesn't bother him. He replies that other kinds of racing simply don't appeal to him, and he prefers staying with what he knows best.

Just how long he will stay with racing is a constant subject of speculation. Sportswriters ask him when he is going to retire at almost every race. He has set all the records, made himself wealthy, they point out, so why go on? What else is there to prove? Every driver knows that the more he races the greater the chance that the day of the final wreck will come, so why continue to face the risk?

Petty laughs and shrugs off the question, pointing out that at his age (he was born in 1937) his father was just beginning to race. Besides, there is all that money, the race purses, the appearance fees (he gets $3,000 just for showing up at the big tracks, $1,500 from the small ones, plus varying amounts for other away-from-the-track appearances), the money from commercial endorsements, and all those people who depend on him (some 35 working for the Petty racing organization alone). Nobody walks away from all of that—not until he has to.

Risk? Well, maybe a little. But he doesn't pay it any attention. No driver does. A driver who worried about risk wouldn't be able to drive.

Richard Petty is a careful race driver. He is known as a driver who "drives with his head," as opposed to a flat-out, stay-in-front-at-all-costs driver. "I don't worry about him," says his wife, Lynda. "I know that *he'll* be careful. It's the other drivers I worry about."

Richard Petty really does not know fear or anxiety, not in the sense that most people do, anyway. During a race, making a movie, appearing on TV, meeting the President, eating supper, playing with his kids—it's all the same to him. He goes about everything in the same way: Take it as it comes, inspect it, decide the best way of going about it, and do the best you can. If anything bothers him, it never shows. He doesn't get scared, excited, or nervous, and he doesn't worry.

"I guess I'm not a very emotional person," he says. "I never have been."

He is, in fact, almost eerily even-dispositioned. It would be hard to imagine what it would take to shake his unemotional, easy-going, level-headed, common-sense approach to life.

Wrecks on racetracks certainly don't do it, and he has had many of those. In the spring of 1970, he survived one of the most spectacular racing wrecks ever seen at Darlington. Coming out of the fourth turn, his car swiped the outside wall, took an abrupt turn to the left, sailed across the track, and smashed almost head-on into the inside wall. It then began a series of end-over-end flips, added a few rolls for good measure, and came to rest on its top, destroyed. Some people who saw the wreck remember it as seeming to happen almost in slow motion. The most vivid part of the memory was seeing Petty's left arm flopping limply outside the window as the car flipped and rolled, and to some it seemed that the car would never come to a stop. Drivers and crew members in the pits ran to the car fully expecting to find Petty dead. He looked dead hanging there in the remains of the car with his limp arm still outside the window. He was taken to the track hospital unconscious, but although badly battered, his worst injury was a dislocated shoulder.

"Hurt my dang shoulder," he told the worried-face doctors when he had regained consciousness.

Later, when he talked with the sportswriters, they asked him what caused the wreck. He grinned.

"I got a little behind in my steerin'," he said.

His even disposition is one of the things that has made Petty an effective spokesman for racing (as well as for a number of products). He does not believe in "bad-mouthing" anybody or anything, but especially racing. He has had his disagreements with NASCAR and with others in racing, and he has let some of his criticisms be known, but he has never spoken out against the sport, and he doesn't like those who do. People who make their livings from racing have a special obligation to support and promote it, he thinks, and he has worked hard to build the image of stock car racing as a "clean" family sport. He probably has done more toward accomplishing that than anybody.

Racing has, or course, been good to him and the other Pettys. It has made them millionares. Petty Enterprises, of which Lee is president, Richard and Maurice vice presidents, not only builds Richard's race cars, but also handles all of Chrysler's racing business, cars and parts, from its Level Cross headquarters. It has also expanded into other fields. The Pettys own a motel, a series of airport warehouses, an interest in a "minority" bank (with blacks and Jews) in Charlotte, widely scattered rental properties, a plastics business, an electronics business, a share in a chain of miniature recreational racetracks, and so on. In addition, Richard Petty is a familiar face on southern television, endorsing everything from hamburgers to "mobile homes" to lawnmowers and soft drinks. And not far from his present home, he is constructing a huge new house on several hundred acres of Randolph County land, where he plans to raise cattle.

Petty takes his hero image seriously. He practices clean living, doesn't drink, is careful of his language, sometimes speaks to church and youth groups, and regularly attends the Methodist church in Randleman when he is not on the road. He is perhaps the biggest supporter of Brother Bill Frazier, who calls himself the chaplain of stock car racing and ministers to racing people. Petty is also quick to give his name, money, and time to any number of good causes . . .

Martinsville lies in the foothills of the Blue Ridge Mountains, and the Martinsville Speedway is set into the side of one of those hills a few miles south of town. It is an immaculate track, probably the finest and most beautiful half-mile track in the country. The grounds are grassed and landscaped, lots of trees, shrubs, and flowers, a pond with geese and ducks. Fences, walls, concession stands, and rest rooms are all whitewashed and kept clean. The concrete grandstands are covered. This was Richard Petty's favorite track, maybe because he had won more races here (twelve) than anybody.

"Hey, there's Richard Petty!"

The race was to start at one, and that was still more than two hours away, but people were already thronging into the track, and they all recognized Richard as he drove slowly past the line of traffic. They called and waved to him, and he waved back. Each car and truck was being stopped at the infield gate, and as he waited his turn, Richard rolled down his window and chatted with a cop about the weather.

The Martinsville infield is tiny and cramped and figure-eight-shaped because of the pit areas that have been cut into it on both sides. It won't hold many cars. Fans who want to get their cars inside must arrive early. By the time the Petty van rolled through the gate, the infield was almost filled. Richard drove slowly toward the top of the eight at the first and second turns, where the Pettys always gather. Cars were already parked four-deep from the fence.

"Don't park on that side," Kyle warned, as his father began to turn toward the backstretch, "you won't win."

"I'm not, I'm just goina back in."

Every time that Richard Petty had won at Martinsville, he had parked in the same area, near the front stretch, and a superstition had grown around it.

Before Richard could get the van parked, a swarm of people was around it, peering closely into the windows, calling his name, aiming their movie cameras, Polaroids, and Instamatics at the van.

"I've done messed up now," he said, looking at all the people. Some were now running from distant areas of the infield. "I should've got out up at the pit gate."

"You'll be lucky to get in there in time for the race," his wife said.

"Where's a pen?" he said, searching around the dashboard. "You gotta pen?"

Lynda handed him a ballpoint pen, and he opened the door smiling to face the people who were already thrusting racing programs, photographs, postcards, autograph books, and scraps of paper at him.

"Sign my shirt, Richard!"

On the first piece of paper, the pen only made an indentation. He bore down, but still it produced no ink.

"Gimme another pen," he said, opening the van door, "that'n there don't write."

"Oh, look at their little baby!" said a woman, breaking for the other side of the van.

While Richard signed autographs with his usual artistic flourish, Lynda opened the side doors of the van and held up the baby for a sizable adoring crowd, who oohed and aahed and snapped pictures for their scrapbooks.

"Ain't she the purtiest little thang!" somebody was saying.

"Richard, do one on my hat," a boy said.

Petty signed the back of the hat while it was still on the wearer's head.

"If you git hit on the back of the head, you'll know why," he told the boy, and turned to sign a girl's proffered arm.

"Pam, you'll just wash that off when you git home," the girl's mother protested.

"I won't neither!"

It took Petty about 15 minutes to make his way to the pit gate, a crowd trailing all the way, and all the way he smiled and bantered amiably.

When he finally made it through the gate, a snaggle-toothed old man called out, "Richard, you better win today, you hear?"

Petty's car occupied the first spot on pit row. His crew was working over the car, putting on the wheels, making last-minute adjustments, waxing again the gleaming finish. Richard huddled for a few minutes with his brother and cousin Dale Inman.

"It's working," Inman said, putting the air breather back in place. "It's working today."

Fifty feet away, people clung to the pit fence calling, "Richard! Hey, Richard Petty!"

A small-town radio announcer thrust a tape recorder microphone into Petty's face and began asking how things looked for the race, and what about the rain?

Petty gave the usual answers that race drivers give to microphones. Things looked pretty good, but then you never know.

"The weather's something we have no control over," Petty was saying to wrap it up . . .

When the green flag dropped, the pack roared into

the first turn at a little over eighty miles per hour with Cale Yarborough, who had started in the pole position, in the lead. Before Yarborough had made it out of the second turn, however, Petty had already jumped two positions to fourth. Yarborough stretched out his lead gradually until he was a half lap ahead, and he seemed to have the fastest car on the track. But at a track like Martinsville, it is skill and not speed that really counts.

It took Petty half the race to jockey into third position. Five laps later, he eased around Bobby Allison into second, and began to close on Yarborough. Petty was losing time in the stretches, but gaining in the turns, and within two laps he was on Yarborough's bumper trying to "root him out of the groove." On the 259th lap, he did it. Yarborough went into the fourth turn too hard, and Petty cut to the inside and sped around him

Lap 340. Caution flag. Buddy Baker and Bobby Allison had bumped in the third and fourth turns, and Baker had skidded out. Petty, still in the lead, made for the pits, Yarborough right behind him. Both took on fresh right-side tires and gasoline, then roared back to make another lap while their crews got ready to replace the left-side tires.

Excitement on the track! Buddy Arrington had pulled away from the pits too soon. A gasoline can was still attached to his car, and one of his wheels was not fully bolted. The wheel came off and the gasoline can caught on fire. Meanwhile, Petty had come back in, with Yarborough still fast on his tail. Their pits were side by side and the crews were now in a frantic race, each hoping to get its car out first. Yarborough's wheels touched the pavement a split second before Petty's and they both spun away, new tires squealing and smoking, but Yarborough had the advantage and won the lead.

For the next 100 laps, Petty fought to regain the lead, never allowing Yarborough to escape the nagging vision in his rear-view mirror of the red-and-blue car hugging his bumper. Occasionally, just as a reminder that he was still back there, Petty would give Yarborough's bumper a tap.

On the 452nd lap, Petty got the break he needed. Something cut Yarborough's right rear tire, causing him to slow just enough for Petty to pull around him. And the rain began to fall again. A few big drops splatted on the windshield seconds after Petty passed. "Let 'er pour!" Petty's jubilant crew members were shouting.

Two laps later, Yarborough, running on the inner liner of his cut tire, came in to replace it, and Petty gained a full lap. The rain had begun to fall harder, and on the 456th lap, the caution flag came out, sealing Petty's position.

"Well, if she just don't fall apart now, we got it," a crew member said.

The cars bunched behind the slow-moving pace car as the rain continued to fall, and on the 480th lap, the red flag finally came out, halting the cars in position. Crew members hurried in to cover the cars with tarpaulins. Petty climbed out of his car and headed toward the control tower at a half run. A couple of his crew members returned to his truck laughing.

"Ol' Richard come out of that car, he said, 'Man, I gotta go pee,'" one of them said . . .

Petty put his jacket, sunglasses, and funny hat back on and stood with his crew members in the back of the truck, waiting to see if the rain would stop so that the last twenty laps could be run. Benny Parsons, the driver who has leading him in the point race for the national championship, crowded into the truck out of the rain.

"Where you been?" Petty asked him.

"You seen me back 'ere, didn't you? Slippin' and a-slidin.'"

Petty sat down in the back of the truck, and after a while the announcement came over the loudspeakers. The race had been called.

"Looks like ever'body's done give up," he said, jumping to the ground.

"Did they call it?" somebody asked from farther back in the truck.

"Didn't they call it?" Petty was saying, a little uncertain now. "Yeah, they called it."

So he had won the 155th race of his career sitting in the back of his truck.

■ ■ ■ ■

Joe Frazier

Three times in the 1970s, all the drama of a turbulent American era was projected onto a pair of men over the course of an hour's athletic contest.

Muhammad Ali was brash, photogenic, and Muslim.

Joe Frazier was hardworking, plain, and polite.

Doves, fellow draft dodgers, and most blacks rooted for Ali, a new kind of African-American.

Hawks and other conservative-leaning folk pulled for Frazier, the white man's black man.

The stakes seemed greater than the boxing matches themselves. No one was neutral.

Half the country laughed when Ali called Frazier an Uncle Tom and a gorilla.

The other half loved it when Frazier used Ali's old name, Cassius Clay.

In truth, Joseph William Frazier was never the establishment tool Ali made him out to be. He was born in 1944 in Beaufort County, South Carolina. The 11th of 12 children of sharecroppers Rubin and Dolly Frazier, he was raised in a tin-roofed house with no telephone, no running water, and an outhouse. Joe's father called him "Billy Boy," the same nickname he used for his Ford truck. Joe worked the family's 10 acres with his father from the age of six or seven. He also rode shotgun and served as lookout while Rubin, a bootlegger and womanizer, delivered whiskey and romanced the ladies. When the truck needed parts, father and son swiped them from the broken-down vehicles of local military personnel.

His uncle Israel, a fight fan, was the one who pushed Joe toward boxing, telling him he could be another Joe Louis. Frazier stuffed a burlap sack with rags, corncobs, and bricks, hung it in the mule stable, and used it as a heavy bag. One day, he broke his left arm while teasing the family's 300-pound razorback. Untreated, it healed with a crook at the elbow. Frazier credits that accident for his signature left hook.

Not long after witnessing a white farmer beltwhip a black boy, the 15-year-old Frazier departed South Carolina alone on a Greyhound bus. He stayed briefly in New York before settling in Philadelphia with an aunt. Just before his 18th birthday, he began visiting the Police Athletic League gym and was discovered by Yancey Durham, who trained him as an amateur fighter. Within two and a half years, he was at the Olympic trials, where he lost to Buster Mathis. After joining the team when Mathis injured his hand, Frazier won heavyweight gold at the 1964 games in Tokyo. Legend says he later had his medal cut into 11 pieces to distribute among his children.

He turned professional in 1965 and won his first four fights by early knockout. The following year, Yancey Durham hired Eddie Futch as an assistant. Though compact, powerful, and relentless, Frazier was not a physical specimen as heavyweights go, standing a little under six feet and weighing slightly more than 205 pounds in his prime. Futch taught Smokin' Joe his distinctive bob-and-weave style to give him greater leverage and make him a tougher target for bigger fighters.

Within a couple of years, Frazier worked his way into contention with victories over the likes of Oscar Bonavena and George Chuvalo. Then as now, boxing's various governing bodies were responsible for a quagmire of competing championships. In 1967, after Ali was stripped of his title for refusing to serve in Vietnam, one boxing faction pit Frazier against Buster Mathis for the heavyweight championship. Joe won by knockout in the 11th round. But he declined on principle to participate in another faction's elimination tournament to crown a replacement for Ali, a competition won by Jimmy Ellis. Ali never properly credited Frazier for that courtesy, or for the financial support Frazier gave him during his exile, or for petitioning President Richard Nixon for Ali's reinstatement.

In 1969 and 1970, respectively, Frazier beat the tough Jerry Quarry and knocked out Jimmy Ellis to consolidate the titles. And then the big fight was on. Since Joe was 26–0 and the reinstated Ali was 31–0, their meeting at Madison Square Garden on March 8, 1971, was the first ever between two undefeated heavyweight champs.

The arena sold out a month in advance. Barbra Streisand, Bill Cosby, Sammy Davis Jr., and Hugh Hefner attended. Diana Ross and Dustin Hoffman were booted from the press section, though Frank Sinatra stayed as a "photographer." Burt Lancaster provided color commentary.

Ali was still feeling the effects of a difficult comeback bout against Oscar Bonavena. Frazier, in top shape, benefited from Eddie Futch's recognition of a flaw in Ali's defenses. Ali was strong in the early rounds, but Frazier staggered him in the 11th and knocked him down in the 15th, both with left hooks, on his way to winning a unanimous decision. Both men spent time at the hospital afterward.

The second Ali-Frazier fight was a non-title bout, Joe having lost his belt in devastating fashion to George Foreman, who floored him six times before the fight was stopped in the second round. In New York in 1974, Ali won a unanimous 12-round decision over Frazier.

Their final fight was the "Thrilla in Manila." This time, Frazier was the challenger and Ali the champion, following his "rope-a-dope" victory over Foreman in the "Rumble in the Jungle" in Zaire. Ali trained lightly, figuring Frazier was washed up. Frazier was incensed at Ali's characterization of him as a dummy and a white man's fighter, feeling he had endured more prejudice over his lifetime than had Ali. Ali initially surprised everyone by going toe to toe with Frazier. Smokin' Joe then won the middle rounds. But once Frazier ran out of energy, Ali beat him so badly that he could barely see from his swollen eyes. Eddie Futch stopped the fight before the 15th round. Frazier never spoke to him again. Ali said that fight was the closest he ever came to dying and conceded Frazier was "the greatest fighter in the world, next to me."

Frazier wound down his career with a loss to Foreman in 1976 and a draw with Jumbo Cummings in 1981.

Today, he runs a gym in Philadelphia. His post-fight life has included a cameo in *Rocky* (the carcass-punching scene is said to have come from Frazier's training), a singing career with Joe Frazier & the Knockouts, a stint as corner man for Mr. T at WrestleMania, and appearances on *The Simpsons*.

Though he has reconciled periodically with Ali, bitter feelings run deep. When Ali lit the Olympic torch in Atlanta, Frazier told a reporter he wished he could throw his old nemesis into the fire. Unfortunately, Frazier will be forever remembered by many as the greatest opponent of "the Greatest." Here's hoping a rise from difficult circumstances and a lifetime of accomplishment are adequate consolation.

—Stephen Kirk

"A Limousine Riding, Jet Flying, Kiss Stealing, Wheeling Dealing, Son of a Gun"

By Tom Sorensen

Ric Flair came to Charlotte almost 40 years ago. He didn't arrive by limousine, but he should have. He was one of the many then. He had come from Minneapolis, where he had grown up the son of a prominent doctor. Instead of medical school, however, Flair chose Verne Gagne's wrestling school. That might have been tougher. Prospective wrestlers were always running up stairs and back down, carrying something or somebody and doing squats. There were always squats. The idea was to run off the pretenders. Every time they thought they were finished, Gagne made them do it again.

After Flair graduated, he left Minneapolis and came south to work for the National Wrestling Alliance. The grapplers gathered in a nondescript building on a nondescript road near a nondescript series of strip malls, ma and pa restaurants, apartment complexes and light industry. Only insiders knew what went on inside.

There were cameras, studios and stars. Walk in and you'd encounter glamorous valets, cowboys, barbarians, aliens that spoke no known language, more blond hair than you'd see at a South Beach bar and evil Russians who shaved their head, called everybody comrade and had never lived outside the Carolinas. There were big men, big women and enormous egos.

This is where I met Flair. I was writing a column about him for the *Charlotte News*, an afternoon paper that would soon merge with the larger *Charlotte Observer*. The wrestlers helped postpone our demise. Before the NBA and NFL came to Charlotte, and before racing evolved from a regional to a national sport, there was wrestling. And readers wanted to read about the wrestlers, even those that spoke no known language.

I figured the Nature Boy, the superstar with the flashy robes, the famous strut and the electric neon hair, would speak loudly, and about himself. All I got was the hair.

He was humble. He talked quietly. He gave me his real name (Richard Fliehr). He asked about my family. He did this in part because he wanted, and still wants, to be liked. But beneath the flash was a man grateful for the opportunities he had been given and grateful for the manner in which his new hometown had taken him in. How many of us get to do the thing we're meant to do? Flair did, and he knew it.

Lastly, I took his sport seriously. I wasn't there to write that the outcome of a match was predetermined. I believe that had been done before.

This was more than 25 years ago, and we've been friends since.

Back then, newspaper reporters had their bars, lawyers had their bars, cops had their bars and wrestlers had their bar. The wrestlers gathered at Bennigan's. And because they did, Charlotte did.

Walk in and there were Wahoo McDaniel and Sting and T.A. Magnum, Baby Doll and the Andersons and Tully Blanchard, the Midnight Express and the Rock 'n' Roll Express. Is that Dusty Rhodes? I believe it is. The bar could have made a profit off the wrestlers, groupies and hangers-on and probably did. These were the biggest stars in Charlotte, and you could not imagine their time coming to an end.

But it came to an abrupt end. Ted Turner purchased the National Wrestling Alliance and moved it to Atlanta, and most of the wrestlers were forced to move with it. The nondescript building out of which the wrestlers worked became even more nondescript and Bennigan's went out of business.

Although Flair continued to wrestle for the NWA, he stayed in Charlotte. The organization needed him more than he needed them. He was now one of the few. And his popularity grew. We appreciated the wrestlers. They made our town more interesting. And he was the last of them and our only connection to our past.

Even when the NBA and NFL came, Flair remained the city's biggest star. He attracted crowds, and sometimes an ovation, when he walked into a bar, a Charlotte Hornets game or Carolina Panthers game. The Panthers put him on the scoreboard at football games and up in Raleigh, the Carolina Hurricanes played his trademark "Woooo" at NHL games.

Michael Jordan is the biggest name in Charlotte but when was the last time somebody saw Michael out? When was the last time, meanwhile, somebody saw Flair anywhere other than out?

Flair draws his strength from crowds. I've seen him, in one night in one restaurant, sign autographs until his hands were numb, pose for pictures with the fellows and flirt with the women at the table near the door, a bridal party, who had started it by flirting with him.

People know that I know him, and they want to tell me stories about him. On a flight back from a Panthers road game, a contractor who used to wrestle said that in the old days none of the wrestlers had insurance. He said he got hurt and had to quit. Flair, he said, walked up, handed him a few hundred dollars, and walked away.

The older Flair became, the bigger he became. A new restaurant had opened in the suburbs, and on Friday nights patrons would wait hours for a table. On one Friday, the line extended out the lobby, out the door and onto the patio outside. Hundreds of people stood out there, one of them Flair.

The general manager saw him, rushed to him and led him into the restaurant. On the way they passed two Panthers, both starters on defense and among the most recognizable athletes in town.

Do you know who they are, Flair asked?

Yes. They're somebody other than Ric Flair.

Flair lobbied, and the general manager went back and plucked them out of the line, too.

Flair left the business once. One of the wrestling organizations for which he worked entrusted the business to an incompetent, and Flair left. I didn't see him for months. I'm not sure anybody did. Maybe being Ric Flair had worn him out.

One day at a suburban mall, the same one with the restaurant at which he rescued the football players, an oversized SUV pulled up.

"Hey, young man," the driver said.

I don't know anybody dumb enough to call me young. And I had never seen the guy before. He was pale, with close cropped salt and pepper hair.

"You don't recognize me do you?" he asked.

Um . . .

"Tom, I'm Ric Flair," he said.

Richard Fliehr, maybe.

The next time I saw him, his hair was long and blond and he was as tan as a Florida golf pro.

Ric Flair was back. You have to be what you are, and Flair is a limousine riding, jet flying, kiss stealing, wheeling dealing, son of a gun who's kissed the girls and made them cry.

When former President George H.W. Bush visited South Carolina, and then Charlotte, on separate occasions, Flair sat with the President at his table. Flair complained that he couldn't afford a third visit because he had already bought his then-wife two gowns.

These days, you aren't likely to turn on the TV and see Flair in a ring. He turned 60 in February, 2009. Wrestling, he can leave. But how do you leave the life?

You don't. So on a cold December Saturday night as 2008 comes to an end there he is in a Charlotte high school gym, managing his professional wrestler sons David and Reid. Flair wears a suit and manages calmly from the corner. The fans that fill the metal folding chairs around the ring and the bleachers beyond it applaud the younger Flairs. But they do not become truly crazed until Flair rips off the jacket and slips between the ropes.

Professional wrestling is, as many of you suspect, pretend. But more than any wrestler I've ever seen Flair makes you want to believe. His amateur background enables him to sell conventional moves, and his fearlessness enables him to appeal to the fans that come to see large bodies sail and crash.

Flair performs. Look at him in the corner, cowering on one knee, asking for forgiveness, now begging for forgiveness, his opponent glowering, Flair promising never again to do the thing he just did. My god, how can you not believe him? Give Ric Flair a chance, O.K.?

As the opponent debates out loud about whether Flair is worthy, the Nature Boy will suddenly plant a finger in the man's eye. And watch out, because if Flair puts you in his signature hold, the figure-four leglock, a maneuver so lethal it was banned in three cities, two towns and all of Nova Scotia, the match ends.

"Ric is the greatest," Hulk Hogan once told me. "Everything about him says he is a wrestler. He even looks like a wrestler."

After the match in the high school gym, fans walked into the gray, cold night and drove off in their trucks and cars.

Flair left in a limo.

"Sweet D"

By David Dickson

While clearing out things for a recent move, I came upon a Converse shoe box filled with old letters, a T-shirt and impossibly small gym shorts. The letters were addressed to David "Sweet D" Dickson, and the shirt and shorts bore the emblem of the Dean Smith Basketball Camp. I wondered why I had lugged those things around for more than 30 years, because I am not much for sentimentality, or holding on to the past. It caused me to consider the nickname on the letters, and what attending basketball camp had meant to me as a kid.

The 1970's was a great decade in Atlantic Coast Conference basketball history. For several summers I attended a week of basketball camp at the University of North Carolina at Chapel Hill, and every time I roomed with the same three buddies, the ones who sent me those letters long ago.

Most of the kids at camp would never even make their high school varsity team, and many were there mostly to obtain autographs from the current and former Tar Heel players in town for the camp. The kids who were too eager for autographs became targets of my disdain. Any time a Tar Heel player walked through the cafeteria in Granville Towers, a gang of campers ran begging the players to sign camp T-shirts, or blue and white basketballs. My group of friends looked down on that type of adulation, and the term "jock sniffers" was used to identify the souvenir seekers.

There was only one Tar Heel player that I held in the highest esteem, and that was Walter Davis. My sister attended UNC in those days, and during her freshman year she lived across the hall from a girl who dated Walter. From the first time I saw him play the game, Walter Davis became my idol. I wanted to shoot like him, to run the floor in the graceful manner that earned him the nickname "the Greyhound," and to be the coolest guy off the court.

My sister would keep me updated each time Walter came to the dormitory. Walter, she said, was a sharp dresser. He pressed his jeans and T-shirts, and always wore new Converses. She told me that his girlfriend said he wore his T-shirts one time before discarding them, and the shoes not many more times than that. Walter's style earned him another nickname, "Sweet D."

My sister related a story about how she and a group of friends were in a bar on Franklin Street called He's Not Here. Walter and his girl showed up after things really got rocking and they came over to the table where my sister and her friends were drinking beer. One of the girls in the group had consumed too many beers and retreated to the bathroom where she became ill. Not long after she excused herself from the table, the girl (who shall remain nameless) heard a kind voice speak her name and a soft touch on her shoulder. She looked up to see Walter Davis and his girlfriend in the women's room. Walter asked if he could help her. The girl could barely respond, so Walter picked her up in his arms and whispered, "Now don't you fro-up on me." After that, Walter Davis was not just my favorite player, he was my hero.

☆ ☆ ☆

In summer of 1977, I was about to turn 14 when Carolina basketball camp opened. It was one year after the United States won the gold medal in the Summer Olympics. Four Tar Heel basketball players were on that team coached by Dean Smith. I was at the end of my innocent years, and the week of camp had been a fun time, but I knew I wasn't going to be attending many basketball camps after that summer. On a sweltering afternoon, my buddies and I walked across campus to Carmichael Auditorium to watch a pick-up game of Tar Heel players. The gym was packed with campers, many swarming the court to beg autographs from the players.

I took a seat on the baseline and waited for the game to begin when Walter Davis glided by looking like the smoothest cat I'd ever seen in my life. He sat on the floor not far from me and began taking off purple warm-up pants. It was my chance to meet my hero. I walked over to Walter and introduced myself, mentioned my sister. Walter was very nice, he looked around the crowded gym, and then asked me if I would keep an eye on his stuff. He handed me the warm-up pants, and took off his shirt, giving them both to me.

I tried to be casual about it, but I couldn't help checking out the gear Walter trusted me to keep. It was a white shirt commemorating the men's basketball gold medal of the 1976 Olympic Games. The purple warm-ups had a flared leg and the emblem of the Phoenix Suns, the NBA team which had drafted Walter that summer. My buddies watched the scene play out and they knew I was feeling on top of the world.

When the game finished, it was time for me to return to Granville Towers for check-in, but Walter Davis was nowhere to be found; he'd left me waiting with the clothes I'd been entrusted to keep safe. The thought occurred to me that I could leave with a very special memento of my all-time favorite player, but I just couldn't do it. I went looking and I found Walter in a hallway talking to a very attractive coed. He accepted the clothes with a smile and a thanks.

The other day when I came upon the old letters and basketball camp shirt and shorts, I'm glad I didn't find a pair of Phoenix Suns warm-ups, or a T-shirt from the 1976 Olympics. It would have made me very sad to admit I'd been a "jock sniffer" myself. This way, sometimes I can still think of myself as David "Sweet D" Dickson.

Dale Earnhardt: The Man in Black

By Sharyn McCrumb

Dale Earnhardt, the Intimidator, the driver of the black number three, was a seven-time NASCAR Winston Cup Series champion, winning 76 Cup races, including the 1998 Daytona 500, in a racing career that spanned 27 years. The only NASCAR driver ever to win the Cup championship the year after winning Rookie of the Year, Dale Earnhardt was an inductee in the Motorsports Hall of Fame, and was named one of NASCAR's 50 Greatest Drivers. His impact on the sport of stock car racing transcends his long list of awards and honors. Earnhardt, a native of Kannapolis, North Carolina, was an average-looking guy with a minimal education, who embodied the dreams of a legion of fans. His death made grown men cry.

Dale Earnhardt died on February 18, 2001, in the last lap of the Daytona 500. For the rest of the 2001 season, at every race thousands of spectators would stand at attention during lap number three, raising three fingers in a silent tribute to their fallen hero. Ironically, the only time Dale Earnhardt ever won the annual fan-chosen "Most Popular Driver Award" was in 2001, posthumously—a gesture echoing the sentiment in an Edwin Arlington Robinson poem, *"I never knew the worth of him until he died."*

☆ ☆ ☆

Dale Earnhardt's rookie year in Cup racing, 1979, ushered him into the sport at a time when NASCAR stopped being the low-paying regional obsession of his father's era, and became a glitzy, media-driven national pastime. His death in the Daytona 500 marked—maybe even *caused*—the jump to light speed that transformed stock car racing from a folksy Southern pastime into a global phenomenon of millionaire rock star-style Cup drivers (like Dale Earnhardt, Jr.), with more than 70 million fans, and speedways from coast to coast.

Ralph Dale Earnhardt was born on April 29, 1951, the third child and eldest son of auto mechanic and stock car driver Ralph Earnhardt (NASCAR Sportsman Champion of 1956) and his wife Martha Coleman, the daughter of a Cabarrus County farm family. Since Kannapolis was a mill town, it was probably harder in those days for a man to escape from a mill job than it was to acquire one. Ralph Earnhardt, who had dropped out of school in his early teens, hired on at the mill where his older brothers worked, but he soon learned that factory work didn't suit him, so a few months after he married Martha Coleman on August 23, 1947, he went to work fixing cars at the garage of Mr. Berlin Edelman, a fellow member of the Center Grove Lutheran Church in Kannapolis. Ralph Earnhardt was not in the moonshine business, but some of the garage customers were, and occasionally Ralph would be assigned to deliver a souped-up car to one of the bootleggers. Road testing these high-powered cars on the delivery run up Highway 421 gave Ralph Earnhardt a yen to try racing, and by the early 1950s he had begun to compete on the local stock car circuit.

Thus Dale Earnhardt grew up in a home where the family business was stock car racing. He spent his childhood in a little white frame house on Sedan Avenue, playing sandlot baseball across the street, and riding his bike, but as he grew older, he began to spend much of his time in the garage behind the house, built by his father as a place to work on his race cars and to do general repair work for cars as a business.

"I never cared much about school," Dale Earnhardt said later in life. "I'd rather be working the shop."

When Ralph Earnhardt raced at the local North Carolina tracks—Hickory, Wilkesboro, Asheville—his three sons, Dale, Randy, and Danny, comprised the pit crew. This apprenticeship taught the Earnhardt boys their way around a car at an early age, but only Dale wanted to become a driver like his father. When Ralph Earnhardt died of a heart attack at age 44 in September 1973, 22-year-old Dale, who had dropped out of school in ninth grade, became the family race car driver (thus far only on dirt track), and thus the new patriarch. By then Dale was divorced from his first wife Latane (mother of Kerry Dale Earnhardt, born December 8, 1968), and married to Brenda Gee (daughter of NASCAR engine builder Robert Gee, Sr.). Brenda Gee is the mother of Kelley Earnhardt Elledge (August 28, 1972) and Dale Earnhardt, Jr. (October 10, 1974). The couple divorced in 1977.

Dale Earnhardt's racing career began much the way his father's had: racing on the small regional tracks throughout the Southeast. In 1974 he was working for Whitaker's Wheel Alignment Shop in Concord, North Carolina, not far from the Charlotte Motor Speedway, and he decided that the only way he would make it to a career in racing was to devote himself to it full-time, so he told his boss he was quitting to be a race car driver.

"You're going to starve to death, boy," the boss told him.

To switch from dirt track racing to asphalt—the only road to NASCAR—Earnhardt bought an old race car from Harry Gant, and began to compete on the regional circuit. He later said that he was glad he had begun his career racing dirt track, because that experience had sharpened his reflexes and taught him to be responsive to the feel of the car.

Dale Earnhardt's first Winston Cup race came in May 1975 at the Charlotte Motor Speedway, where he started 33rd and finished 22nd. From 1975 to 1977, Earnhardt drove Sportsman races and an occasional Winston Cup race when he could persuade someone to let him drive. In 1978, when he was reduced to borrowing money for tires and engines, he kept looking for the big break in racing, while his mounting debts threatened to cost him his racing equipment and his chance at the big time.

The break came in the fall of 1978, thanks to West Coast businessman Rod Osterlund, a new Cup team owner from whom Earnhardt had been buying used parts. Some of Osterlund's shop guys, with whom Dale had become friends, suggested to Osterlund that the team should field a car for Earnhardt to drive. Since they didn't have a car available, the shop guys offered to build him one. They rebuilt a wrecked Chevrolet Monte Carlo, and, although the car did not handle well, Earnhardt was outrunning Dave Marcis, the Osterlund team's regular driver. The transmission gave way with 10 laps to go but Earnhardt stayed out and finished second to Bobby Allison. At the end of the season, Dave Marcis told the team that he would not return for the '79 season. Earnhardt had raced well at Atlanta and finished 11th at Ontario, California, so Earnhardt was offered the full-time ride in the blue and yellow Osterlund Chevrolet.

He was on his way.

☆ ☆ ☆

Early in Earnhardt's rookie season of Cup racing, the Osterlund team hired Jake Elder to be crew chief for their new driver. Elder, the former crew chief of Darrell Waltrip, was good at grooming novice drivers for the competitive Cup circuit. Elder guided Earnhardt to his first Cup win, the 1979 spring race at Bristol. It was his only win of the season, perhaps because a wreck at Pocono fractured both of Earnhardt's collar bones, causing him to sit out four races, while David Pearson filled in for him and won the Southern 500 at Darlington. Despite missing those races, though, Earnhardt won Rookie of the Year honors, with the best ever rookie season in NASCAR—four poles and a win—making him the first NASCAR rookie ever invited to compete in the International Race of Champions (IROC). Dale Earnhardt signed a five-year contract with Rod Osterlund, confident that his future in racing was set.

In the 1980 season, Wrangler signed on as the primary sponsor for the Osterlund car, and "Suitcase" Jake Elder, who never stayed long anywhere, left the team, so Earnhardt went from having one of the most experienced crew chiefs in NASCAR to having the most inexperienced one—21-year-old California native Doug Richert. However, in a hard-fought points race with Cale Yarborough, who had announced his retirement, Dale Earnhardt won his first NASCAR championship by nineteen points.

The 1981 season opened with Richard Petty winning his seventh victory in the Daytona 500, thanks to the fuel strategy of his cousin and long-time crew chief Dale Inman. Weeks later, Inman announced that he was leaving the Petty team to become chief of operations for the Osterlund team. For the first half of the season, Earnhardt's luck on the track was all bad. Then in June Rod Osterlund announced that he was selling the team to Jim Stacy, whose reputation in NASCAR circles was not good. Stacy indicated that it didn't matter to him if either Earnhardt or Wrangler stayed on board or not. After first talking to team owner Junior Johnson, who could not offer Dale a ride at that time, driver and sponsor met with owner-driver Richard Childress, who made what he called "the hardest decision of his life"—to give up being a driver himself—knowing that the influx of big money into stock car racing had changed the sport forever, and the era of small-time owner/drivers was over. Earnhardt and Wrangler went over to Richard Childress, and for the rest of the season they struggled, losing races and money, and ending the '81 season without a win. Richard Childress, mindful that he was hampering the career of a Cup champion, made the unselfish decision to release Earnhardt, advising him to find a team that had the money and personnel to give him a competitive car.

In 1982 Earnhardt drove a Ford for Bud Moore, winning at Darlington, but because of engine problems and crashes, he failed to finish 18 events out of 30.

On November 14, 1982, Dale Earnhardt married Teresa Houston, whose father and uncle were both race car drivers. She understood the life on the racing circuit, and she had been his friend through the hard times in his career, often looking out for Dale Jr. and Kelley at the track while their father was racing. The couple had one daughter, Taylor Nicole, born December 20, 1988.

The happiness in Earnhardt's personal life contrasted with professional turmoil in the '83 racing season, which ended with his resignation from the Bud Moore team. A deal was struck so that Earnhardt replaced Ricky Rudd as the driver for Richard Childress, while Rudd took his ride on the Bud Moore team, with Wrangler paying partial sponsorship money to both. Earnhardt and Childress were back together, a partnership that would endure for the rest of Dale Earnhardt's life.

☆ ☆ ☆

Although Earnhardt founded his own racing team, Dale Earnhardt Incorporated (DEI), located on what is now N.C. Route 3 in Mooresville, Dale Earnhardt himself drove the black number three for Richard Childress Racing from 1984 until his death in 2001. The combination of the black paint scheme and Earnhardt's aggressive driving style earned him the nickname the Intimidator, and made him a larger-than-life player on the NASCAR stage. People either loved him or hated him.

RCR and Earnhardt went on to win six more NASCAR Cup Championships (in 1986, 1987, 1990, 1991, 1993, 1994), tying the all-time championship record of Richard Petty.

In 1988 GM Goodwrench replaced Wrangler as the full-time sponsor on the #3, changing the #3 Monte Carlo's paint scheme to black and silver, so that for the remaining 13 years of his racing career, Dale Earnhardt was "the man in black."

The one achievement that eluded Dale Earnhardt for most of his career was the winning of the Daytona 500. Every year since 1979 he would go out, often in the best car, often having won several races at the Daytona track during the week, and still he would lose the race that counted. Ironically, Earnhardt holds the sport's record for the most wins at Daytona International Speedway—his total in all three divisions of NASCAR give him 29 victories there. From 1990 through 1994 Earnhardt won the Grand National Race at Daytona, which took place the day before the Cup race—and still he would lose on Sunday. The causes for his losses included almost every possible way to snatch defeat from the jaws of victory: pit stop problems with a fuel nozzle ('87); running over track debris and crashing ('90); running out of gas in the last lap ('86). People said that if the race was the Daytona 499, he would win every year, but some misfortune, usually occurring in the last lap, always denied him the long-awaited win.

In 1994 Earnhardt's best friend, Alabama driver Neil Bonnett, was killed during a Daytona 500 practice session on the track. The next year, after winning the mid-week 125-mile qualifying race for the Daytona 500, Earnhardt said: "Ol' Neil Bonnett rode with me today, and he is going to ride with me to a win in the 500."

It was not to be.

He won the 125-mile qualifying race during Speed Week at Daytona, and then the 100-lap IROC race, but in the 1995 Daytona 500, without drafting help and stopping for fresh tires in hopes of making a run on race leaders Mark Martin and Sterling Marlin, Earnhardt—despite the fans' expectations and his encouraging weeklong successes—lost the race to Sterling Marlin, who won it for the second straight year. In interviews afterward, a frustrated Dale Earnhardt told reporters, "This is the Daytona 500. I am not supposed to win the damned thing."

In 1998 Earnhardt changed his luck and gave stock car racing a new legend: The Lucky Penny Story. On February 15, 1998, Earnhardt was at the track hours before the start of the race, and a sick child was brought to see him. Six-year old Wessa Miller of Pikeville, Kentucky, was a Dale Earnhardt fan, and when she met her hero, she told him that he would win the race that day. She gave him a "lucky penny," and assured him that the coin would bring him victory. After 19 straight losses in this race, Dale Earnhardt must have figured that he needed all the help he could get. Before the race began, he duct-taped the little girl's lucky penny to the dashboard of his #3 Goodwrench Chevrolet.

On lap 198 Earnhardt was leading the race, when the cars of John Andretti and Lake Speed made contact, causing the race to end under a caution flag, with Earnhardt as the winner. After his win, he made a triumphant procession down pit road, where the crews of all the race teams were lined up to shake his hand and congratulate him on the momentous win.

The driver of the black number three lived for three years and three days after his victory in the Daytona 500, dying in the last lap of the race, 11 seconds from the finish line.

The race had been red-flagged following an 18-car wreck on lap 173, and after the restart, the race leaders were two DEI drivers, Michael Waltrip and Dale Earnhardt Jr., and the black #3 of Dale Earnhardt. On turn three of the last lap of the race, Earnhardt was running three-wide between the #36 Pontiac of Ken Schrader and Sterling Marlin. Marlin's front bumper made contact with the left rear fender of the #3, causing Earnhardt's car to slide off the banked track and onto the apron, and then to veer sharply back up the track toward the outside wall. As it neared the wall, there was a collision between Earnhardt's car and Schrader's, sending both cars nose first into the wall, and killing Dale Earnhardt instantly.

After an autopsy, doctors announced that the cause of death was a basilar skull fracture. His safety harnesses had not provided sufficient restraint to protect his spinal cord from trauma in the 160 mph crash.

The winner of the race was Michael Waltrip, driving the #15 car for Dale Earnhardt Incorporated. Richard Childress announced that the number 3 would be retired from RCR racing, and that a different paint scheme would be applied to the GM Goodwrench car, which was assigned the number 29, and was driven by Kevin Harvick, who scored his first Cup series win at Atlanta three weeks after Earnhardt's death.

Dale Earnhardt became the fourth driver to die in a motorsports accident since the death of Adam Petty on the track in New Hampshire in 2000. This mounting death toll, plus the anguish of millions at the loss of their hero, resulted in a number of safety reforms in racing. After Earnhardt's death, NASCAR began to require that the HANS device, a head and neck restraint, be used to protect drivers from the sort of spinal cord injury that had caused Earnhardt's death. Oval tracks on the racing circuit installed *SAFER* barriers to reduce the impact trauma during crashes. NASCAR inspection teams became more vigilant about seat belt requirements and safety inspections, and in 2007 they introduced the Car of Tomorrow, a redesigned car for Cup racing that was intended to improve driver safety. Among the innovations in the boxier new stock car: moving the driver's seat to the right by four inches, and shifting the roll cage three inches toward the rear. In the eight years since Dale Earnhardt died, there have been no on-track deaths in NASCAR Cup racing.

On February 15, 2004, six years to the day after Dale Earnhardt's winning of the Daytona 500, his son Dale Earnhardt, Jr., also won the race. Six years after Earnhardt's death, Kevin Harvick, still in the #29 GM Goodwrench car for RCR, won the Daytona 500.

Dale Earnhardt still continues to be a presence in NASCAR, with sales of his memorabilia ranking in the top three among drivers. He has been memorialized in the 2004 film *#3: The Dale Earnhardt Story*, starring Barry Pepper as Dale Earnhardt, and in a 2007 documentary titled *Dale*. His hometown of Kannapolis, North Carolina, named a street Dale Earnhardt Boulevard, which begins at exit 60 off Interstate 85. In Mooresville, NC, Highway 136, which runs past Dale Earnhardt Incorporated, was renamed North Carolina Route 3 in his honor. At Daytona International Speedway a seating section was named in honor of Dale Earnhardt, and near the entrance to the main building is a bronze statue of a smiling Dale Earnhardt, holding the Harley Earle trophy of his Daytona 500 victory.

Michael Jordan

How ubiquitous was Michael Jordan during his heyday?

In 1989, 1993, and 1998, respectively, he claimed the most coveted photo placement in athletics—the cover of *Sports Illustrated*—playing golf, baseball, and cards.

How pervasive is his influence today?

Watch a basketball game anywhere from Beaufort to Bucharest to Beijing, on any level from peewee to professional, boys' or girls', men's or women's, fully able or wheelchair-bound. Pay attention to number 23. That's the hotshot.

Jordan was born in Brooklyn in February 1963 and moved with his family to Wilmington, North Carolina, as a toddler. He was cut from the varsity team at E. A. Laney High School as a sophomore before growing four inches over the summer and scoring 25 points per game his final two years. As a senior, he averaged a triple-double—29 points, 12 rebounds, and 10 assists—and was selected to the McDonald's All American Team.

If you don't know the story of Jordan's first season at the University of North Carolina, you don't follow basketball. He averaged 13.4 points on 53.4 percent shooting and was the ACC Freshman of the Year. Then came the national championship game against Georgetown and Patrick Ewing, a freshman even more precocious—to that point, anyway. With 17 seconds left and Carolina down by one, Coach Dean Smith turned to Jordan and uttered the fateful words, "Knock it down, Michael"—this to a skinny freshman on a team boasting Sam Perkins and James Worthy.

Even if you're not Smith's biggest fan, you have to admire his prescience. Michael hit a 17-footer and, after an inadvertent handoff from Georgetown's Fred Brown to Worthy, Carolina won 63–62.

Jordan acknowledges that shot as a major factor in his development. He returned the following season stronger and more assertive. Smith once said he never saw a player improve as much as Jordan did between his freshman and sophomore years. He didn't even need his prescience to notice that. The change was obvious. When Jordan averaged a little under 20 points per game his next two seasons, Smith's system was said to be holding him back. He left college in 1984 after his junior year and was drafted third by the Chicago Bulls, behind Akeem Olajuwon and injury-addled Sam Bowie.

He majored in cultural geography, by the way. He finished his studies in 1986.

An NBA patsy after going 27–55 in the 1983–84 season, the Bulls were suddenly the hottest ticket in basketball. Jordan averaged a remarkable 28.2 points his rookie year and then—after sitting out 64 games the following season with a foot injury—an even more remarkable 37.1 points his third year. But the Bulls couldn't get over the hump, falling to Larry Bird's Boston Celtics in Jordan's second and third seasons and to Isiah Thomas' "Bad Boy" Detroit Pistons the three years after that.

The breakthrough came in the 1990–91 season. The Bulls swept the Pistons in the conference finals, the jealous Thomas—the same player who had refused to pass Jordan the ball during Michael's first All Star game—pulling his team off the floor before the fourth game concluded. Jordan led the Bulls past the Lakers in the finals, then past Portland in the finals the following year. The Bulls completed their three-peat in 1992–93, Jordan averaging a finals-record 41 points in a six-game triumph over the Suns.

Jordan's next two years combined the bizarre and the tragic. He was worn out from nonstop basketball, having led the Dream Team at the Olympics in Barcelona the previous summer. And then accusations of a gambling problem arose during the NBA playoffs in 1993. And then that July, his father, James Jordan, was murdered along the road near Lumberton, North Carolina. Two and a half months later, Jordan announced his retirement from basketball at age 30. Conspiracy theorists maintain he was under some kind of super-secret gambling suspension from the NBA.

He didn't go quietly. Rather, Jordan became to professional baseball what Jim Brown, another great early retiree, was to acting. As an outfielder for the AA Birmingham Barons, an affiliate of the Chicago White Sox, Jordan proved error-prone and weak at the plate, batting just .202.

In March 1995, after a year and a half out of basketball, Jordan issued a two-word statement: "I'm back." He joined the Bulls for their stretch run, wearing a new jersey, number 45. When Chicago fell to Shaquille O'Neal's Magic in the playoffs, Orlando's Nick Anderson said that number 45 just "didn't look like the old Michael Jordan."

The rest of the league soon regretted that statement. Chicago and the rejuvenated Jordan, again wearing number 23, went an NBA-record 72–10 in the 1995–96 season and beat Seattle for the championship, then defeated Utah in the finals each of the next two years for another three-peat.

In early 1999, facing an owners' lockout and the expiring contract of Coach Phil Jackson, Jordan retired a second time. A year later, he was back as president of basketball operations for the Washington Wizards. A year and a half after that, in September 2001, he took the court for the Wizards. He played two seasons in his third go-round. The Wizards fired him from his front-office job three weeks after his final game as a player.

He is now part-owner and managing member of basketball operations for the Charlotte Bobcats.

Over his career, Jordan was a memory-making machine—the shot over Craig Ehlo, the push-off against Bryon Russell, the switch-handed scoop, the foul-line dunks, the "HORSE" commercials with Larry Bird, even the tongue-wagging.

But even if Jordan is Superman, he's no Solomon. His shallow statement when declining to endorse Harvey Gantt over Jesse Helms in the 1990

Senate race—"Republicans wear sneakers, too"—left most observers wishing UNC's cultural geography curriculum had a stronger civics component. And Jordan's indifferent management and poor personnel judgment with the Wizards and Bobcats have placed him at the bottom of NBA administrators—right alongside his old buddy Isiah Thomas.

Still, it's hard to argue with six NBA championships, two Olympic gold medals, 14 All Star appearances, a career scoring average of 30.1, a third-place standing on the NBA's scoring list, five MVP awards, and a Defensive Player of the Year award. Jordan's adoring public has reaped a couple of nicknames ("Air Jordan," "His Airness"), an adjective ("Jordanesque"), several "Next Jordans" (Vince Carter, Kobe Bryant, LeBron James, etc.), one "Baby Jordan" (Harold Miner), numerous sneaker and apparel lines, a ridiculous movie (*Space Jam*), and a new crime (shoe-jacking). Not just his Bulls teammates but the entire basketball universe was indeed Michael Jordan's "supporting cast."

Hey, it's not bragging if you can back it up.

—STEPHEN KIRK

A Special Athlete

By Ann Campanella

For months, my brother Richard had talked about nothing but the Special Olympics World Games. I've always loved the Olympics, but had no idea the Special Olympics had its own version. In 1999, the Special Olympics World Games were to be held in Raleigh, North Carolina. Richard would join with thousands of other mentally handicapped athletes from around the globe. They would participate in the opening and closing ceremonies, stay in dorms on local college campuses, be invited to dances with big-name bands all week long. It promised to be a dream experience.

☆ ☆ ☆

Richard was selected as one of two athletes from Orange County, North Carolina, to compete in the Games. His sport is golf. For weeks, he has been photographed and interviewed by newspapers, television and radio stations; there are parties and cookouts to celebrate the athletes. A friend of mine tells me she saw a life-size photograph of him in a Harris Teeter grocery store. When the family information packet arrives, I order badges for my siblings and myself. It's unusual for us to be in one place at the same time and to plan something around Richard, but this is a big event.

Upon our arrival at Prestonwood Country Club, one of the volunteers directs us to the starting tent. I spot Richard's familiar form. His head is down as if he is a shy spectator while his opponent, Ted, takes practice swings on the tee. Every few seconds Richard adjusts the brim of his cap and his eyes dart toward the clubhouse.

"Hey, Richard!" my brother, Will says. "You've hit the big time."

"Hey, Will." Richard waves and a smile slowly spreads across his face as he sees me and Rose. He offers his palm for a handshake, but Will's arms go around him. Even in the embrace, Richard's hand stays out like a rudder. I reach over and give his fingers a squeeze.

In the 90-degree heat, we follow Richard from hole to hole as he strides around the golf course. As his small gallery, we clap when he hits a good tee shot and shout *hooray* when his putts roll in. Rose offers him water, I take his picture, and Will shakes hands with his coach and caddy. Richard's tee shots don't go far, but they split the fairway. After the first hole he has the honor. He hits his ball, then stands quietly as his opponent whiffs. "Good shot," he says, when Ted finally makes contact.

Each time they reach the green, Richard putts, lifting one foot in anticipation as the ball rolls toward the hole. When it goes in, he raises his fist like a gentle cousin of Tiger Woods. When it doesn't, he cocks his head. "Oh, well."

I think of the hours my father spent with Richard on the golf course. My brother would take three practice swings, then stand over his ball for an eternity. "Keep your head down and follow through," Daddy would say, never losing his patience. Like a wind-up doll with a low battery, Richard's club moved slowly through the air, the club head arcing over his head. There was a *crack* when he hit the ball, and it skittered forty or fifty yards through the grass. My father followed the ball with his eyes. "That was good," he'd say. "You hit it right down the middle."

My father had been a natural athlete, someone who liked to win. But on the golf course with Richard, he became a teacher and an encourager, someone who valued the spirit and essence of his son. And Richard, who was deprived of oxygen at birth, learned that he was someone of worth.

As we walk up the fairway of the ninth hole, Will points, "Look, Richard. You're on the leader board!" We all look up.

A billboard, with the name "Richard Williams" in black letters, stands at the back of the ninth green. Richard isn't in the lead, but it doesn't matter. The volunteers put each golfer's name on the top of the board as they finish their last hole. Richard straightens his shoulders as he stares at the sign.

"It's just like the U.S. Open," I whisper.

He adjusts his cap. "Yes, it is," he says solemnly. At the award ceremony Richard is presented with a ribbon for finishing fourth in his flight. On the stage, his hands clasp his side and his upper body tilts left. As I snap the camera, I motion for him to straighten up. Richard's smile widens and he leans further left.

The family joins my brother for lunch on the North Carolina State University campus. I am surprised at how quiet the cafeteria is. Athletes sit at long tables with their coaches. A few of them have medals around their necks. I expect to see a sense of joy and camaraderie among the groups. Occasional laughter bubbles up from kids with Down Syndrome. But most of the athletes simply focus on their plates of food.

We pepper Richard with questions. He says there have been parties and dances every evening. I want details. But the most I get out of Richard is that he has to get up every morning at 6 AM. When I ask if it was exciting to be with all those athletes from other countries, he says he had to sit in the stadium for four hours and that the opening ceremony was so hot he thought he might pass out.

I've never seen a plate of ravioli and string beans disappear so slowly. I'm not sure if my brother is tired or if he knows that when the meal is over we will be gone. His hand shakes slightly as he brings his fork to his mouth. Rose, Will and I crowd around Richard, hugging him, patting his back and telling stories about his golf round. Richard smiles. The only audience he ever cared about was his family. These Olympics are special because we are here.

Ryan Newman's Canine Connection

By Kris Johnson

Dog lovers probably recognize *Marley & Me* as the title of a non-fiction bestseller based on the life of a beloved pooch bearing that name.

"Harley & Me" could be the name of Daytona 500 winner Ryan Newman's book, should he ever choose to write one. To be fair, though, Newman would have to pen several, given his lifelong love of dogs and chosen avocation.

Newman and his wife, Krissie, have four dogs of their own—Harley being "Daddy's girl"—and the couple pledged $400,000 to launch the recently opened Ryan Newman Foundation Spay/Neuter Clinic in Hickory, N.C. The clinic will serve eight counties and offer low-cost sterilization surgeries for humane societies and other rescue groups who spay and neuter homeless pets before they are adopted. After opening in December, the clinic spayed 131 pets during its first week of operation alone.

Newman's victory in 2008's 50th running of the Daytona 500—followed by a whirlwind media tour including stops on national network shows "Late Show with David Letterman" and "Live with Regis and Kelly"—only helped elevate his philanthropic platform.

Newman's foundation was launched in 2005 with animal welfare as a primary area of focus. He says 4 million to 6 million animals each year are abandoned or sent to shelters nationally and as many as half are euthanized.

"There's 2–3 million innocent lives each year that can be saved if we help control their population," he says.

In ways both large and small, Newman is doing his part.

Each of the past two years, Newman and fellow Sprint Cup driver Greg Biffle have used a trip to Loudon, N.H., to do more than race. The duo has transported dogs slated to die from shelters in North Carolina to New Hampshire. Jodi Geschickter, wife of JTG Daugherty Racing co-owner Tad Geschickter, spearheaded the relocation effort, and six dogs have been saved in the process.

"Thankfully, we were able to rescue those dogs that would have been euthanized due to overpopulation," Newman says.

Newman traces his affinity for dogs back to a childhood spent growing up in rural Indiana. His father,

Originally published in NASCAR Scene, *February 2008.*

Greg, was a hunter, and the family's German shorthairs were originally used for the pursuit of pheasant.

Newman says after he and his sister, Jamie, were born, "Hunting kind of went to the wayside."

The dogs, though, remained as pets.

In addition to the purebred hunters and a black Labrador retriever named Misty the family had for 16 years, Newman specifically recalls a yellow Lab of indeterminate mix named Lady. As the only "non-trophy dog" he can remember in the Newman family, which raised its own beef, Lady left a lasting impression on Ryan.

"She would actually go out there with a good size stick—a four-inch log—and play tug of war with the cow. The cow would put the log in its mouth, and she'd put the log in her mouth, and it was amazing to watch. Things like that make good memories," he says.

Today, it's another Lab of dubious lineage—perhaps with some pit bull or boxer in her—that helps make new memories for Newman: Harley.

"She's very needy. She loves attention. You can stop petting her, and she'll just sort of tackle you," Newman says. "I've always had a love for dogs, just wanted to play with them out in the yard, roll around out in the grass and go do things with them."

Canines have always been constant companions for Newman with one glaring exception: when he ventured to North Carolina in 2001 to chase his NASCAR dream on a full-time basis. It was around then that he met Krissie Boyle, and what ensued was a case of, well, puppy love.

"That was a good fit. When I moved down, I didn't have a dog and lived by myself and wanted to eventually get one. When I met her, I got Digger. Sometimes I tell people when I met Digger, I got Krissie," Newman says.

Clearly, he met his match in more ways than one.

Krissie already had Digger. Together she and Ryan then found Harley in a store parking lot. Harley and Digger discovered Mopar, and Socks was later added to the mix as the family's fourth dog.

Ryan says, "Without a doubt, we treat them as family. If we were to call them kids, we wouldn't be far off."

The book *Pit Road Pets*—a Ryan Newman Foundation-backed project that featured several NASCAR drivers and saw 100 percent of its net proceeds donated to help fund the new complex in Hickory—revealed how many people in the sport are touched by the companionship of animals.

"It's been a very big eye-opener with our book to see how many people in the garage area are affected by a dog or a cat, either through their lives with a story they remember or currently," Ryan says.

Bob Barker, longtime host of "The Price is Right," used to sign off from each television broadcast with a reminder for people to have their pets spayed or neutered. While rescue efforts are admirable, Newman is quick to make the point that spay/neuter activities are vital in the battle against overpopulation.

"We're trying to help rescue the animals, but the ideal thing is to be able to eliminate the overpopulation so we don't have to put ourselves in that situation. We enjoy it, don't get me wrong, but we're only crutching the situation. We need to perform a little surgery," he says.

With Ryan and Krissie serving as national spokespersons for the Humane Alliance's National Spay/Neuter Response Team, the aim is to spread the prevention gospel throughout America.

"It's hard when you've got a new idea and you're trying to bring it to really rural areas," Krissie says.

On a positive note: Having the Daytona 500 champion on your side can only help the cause.

4
THE COACHES

The Coach in the Basement

From *To Hate Like This Is to Be Happy Forever: A Thoroughly Obsessive, Intermittently Uplifting, and Occasionally Unbiased Account of the Duke-North Carolina Basketball Rivalry*

By Will Blythe

Soon after I returned to Chapel Hill, I had arranged to visit with Dean Smith, the former North Carolina head coach. I dressed up for the occasion, although these days the journalist in me had become so blasé about interviews that he tended to walk out of the house wearing whatever happened to be hanging on the nearest chair. But for Smith, I chose a dark, pinstriped suit, the sort you'd wear for an audience with the Pope, if you were the kind of guy who actually wanted to see a Pope.

As I drove across town to the Smith Center on a bright and shining winter noon, it was clear enough that the world hadn't ended at 3 PM on Thursday, October 9, 1997, but it had sure felt that way to me at the time. That was the moment when Smith stepped down after 36 years as coach of the University of North Carolina's men's basketball team. As a Tar Heel expatriate doing hard time in Manhattan, I'd dreaded the day for years, and when Smith announced his retirement, it felt awful, worse even than losing to Duke, though for the record I am compelled to note that that had happened only once in Smith's last nine games against the Blue Devils. Since then . . . well, let's not talk about it.

Phil Ford, the former All-American point guard and then an assistant coach for the Tar Heels, captured the shock and melancholy of Smith's depature when he said that it was "like dying." He was right. In fact, I'd lost relatives with less disruption to my world.

Dean Smith made basketball a religion in our family, rivaled only by Presbyterianism, barbecue, and the Democratic Party. For many years, our dream scenario had gone something like this: Dean beats archrival Duke and its coach, the detested Mike Krzyzewski, for the national championship in April, then runs for the Senate (for which he had been long rumored to be a candidate) and whips the antediluvian Jesse Helms in November! Then we all eat barbecue from Allen & Sons, on Highway 86, to celebrate. Then we go to church to thank God for sending us the wry Kansan to make our state safe for hoops and liberals. Sadly, this never happened.

By the time he retired, he'd won 879 games, more than any other coach in NCAA Division I history. Since taking over the head spot from the charismatic Frank McGuire in the 1961–1962 season, he led Carolina to two national championships, 11 Final Fours,

---

EDITOR'S NOTE: *This excerpt is condensed from a longer chapter in Blythe's book.*

and 13 ACC Tournament championships. Under Smith, the Tar Heels won at least 20 games for each of the 27 straight seasons, 30 of his final 31. In 1976, he coached the Olympic team that restored the gold medal to the United States. In 1983, he was inducted into the Naismith Memorial Basketball Hall of Fame. He had been selected by ESPN as one of the top five coaches of the twentieth century in any sport. In 1998, he received the Arthur Ashe award for courage. And his teams had graduated more than 96 percent of their lettermen. With Smith, we got to applaud not just victories, but a steadfast moral vision. It might have made us, his admirers, a little insufferable from time to time.

☆ ☆ ☆

Over the years, we had studied him intensely. He was something of a stern mystery, a Midwestern preacher-coach thriving in the honeysuckled extravagance of the South, a play-it-close-to-the-vest Kansan whose propriety and saintly soul never quite concealed the capabilities of an assassin. He put sportswriters to sleep with his monotonic poor-mouth (yes, we, too, respected St. Mary's of the Blind, but we knew that on any given night they couldn't really beat us, despite Dean's caution). He could be something of a pious sandbagger. But you listened to him anyway, for the occasional truth he couldn't quite hold back, like when he announced to the world that Duke's two white stars from the late Eighties and early Nineties, Danny Ferry and Christian Laettner, had lower combined SAT scores than those of J.R. Reid and Scott Williams, two black players who were often the brunt of jokes by the Cameron Crazies; "J.R. 'Can't' Reid," they chanted during one game.

It wasn't that we didn't have our criticisms of El Deano (as we affectionately called him, though not to his face). He could be obstinate. In the pre-shot-clock era, he resorted too soon to the four corners, his brilliant delay game, requiring kinesthetic marvels like James Worthy and Michael Jordan to stand around, holding the ball. To the day he retired, his teams appeared to defend the three-point shot as if it were still worth only two points. His hoarding of timeouts turned us into amateur psychologists, speculating on his upbringing. What had he been denied at an early age? He substituted too much, and showed faith in reserves who seemed astonished themselves to be out on the court at crunch time.

In 1993, near the end of the nerve-wracking championship game against Michigan in the New Orleans Superdome, Smith inserted several subs, including the little-used senior guard Scott Cherry. I remember rising in my seat, wondering in unison with thousands of other disbelieving Carolina fans, "What is Dean doing?"

But as usual, Dean's ploy worked. He got his starters some vital rest, and they played sensationally in the final seconds.

We could criticize him, of course, because we loved him. I wondered if we would ever see his like in college sports again. In fact, his type was disappearing from the world faster than rain forests. He was that admirable paradox: the authoritarian liberal, the progressive who wasn't a moral relativist. He treated all of his players equally. He ran a clean program. He helped integrate Chapel Hill restaurants. He supported a nuclear freeze. And he practiced Christianity quietly without the rabid proselytizing so common among the bounty-hunting Christians of today. He emphasized the virtues of tolerance, persistence, and respect.

Sometimes, his rules seemed almost niggling; if a player was late for a team meal before a game, he was held out of the game for exactly the amount of time he was late. It was one of his many lessons in responsibility to your coaches and teammates. But Smith never forgot that responsibility was a two-way street. You weren't just responsible to him. He was responsible to you.

And unlike most present-day liberals—how strange that the label has become so disdained—El Deano won. He won a lot. Just ask that Republican Mike Krzyzewski.

It was ironic, I confess, given all of the above, that I had gone to visit Dean Smith to ask not only about Duke and North Carolina, but also about learning how to lose. But this was the sort of information that middle age demanded. I figured Smith had to know a little something about losing, or long ago, he would have been poisoned from internal pressure like a diver with the bends. Admittedly, there was a paradox here; only the fact that Dean won so much underwrote his opinions about loss.

My trip to the mountain ended in a basement. For that is where I found Dean Smith—in the basement of the Dean E. Smith Center—the basement of his very own building. Ah, the contrasts were too easy to draw: Duke's Mike Krzyzewski on the top floor of his admission-by-scanner-only stone tower, the pine-needled light shining through the high windows; Dean Smith in his basement under a maze of pipes and ducts, a fluorescent world of cinder blocks and concrete floors, of dollies and spare seats and forklifts, in which he had shared a windowless suite with his longtime assistant and brief successor, Bill Guthridge. On the wall of the outer office hung a Bruce Springsteen concert poster.

The cynics might call this self-effacement gaudy in its own way, conspicuous inconspicuousness. The true believers would regard the choice of location as consistent with Smith's nearly Quaker modesty, his aversion to the growing American predilection for self-promotion. He showed what he thought about the trappings of success by moving into a cave underneath his own dome.

Smith met me with a can of Diet Coke in his hand. In contrast to my tributary apparel, he was casually dressed. His hair was whiter, but his famous nose still splayed the air like an ice cutter slicing through the Northwest Passage. He had once received mail from a North Carolina State fan addressed simply to "Coach Nose, Chapel Hill."

Smith had a twinkling way of deflecting the expectations generated by his status of an icon. He asked me about people we knew in common, told me how much a friend of his had respected my father. He proved remarkably unassuming, but why would I have expected anything less of this particular man?

The passionate nature of the rivalries between the North Carolina schools surprised Smith when he first arrived at UNC. "Coming from the Air Force Academy," he said, "I didn't expect anything like this." He attributed the ferocity partly to the strong personalities of McGuire and North Carolina State's Everett Chase, the Indiana native. McGuire was a flamboyant Irish-Catholic from New York who wore custom-made suits with handkerchiefs in their pockets, and who dined at posh restaurants without much concern for who paid. Taking the North Carolina job in 1952, he delighted the locals the way Jim Valvano would do one day at NC State. That is to say, he won, and he was a spectacle.

Case was an Indiana native, a lifelong bachelor looked after by his maid. He arrived in Raleigh in 1946 and began to popularize basketball in his new state. Up to that point, the sport had been merely a bridge between football and baseball, something to occupy what was then a mostly agricultural region after the tobacco had been sold at auction and the farmers were lying low until spring. Case, too, won a lot. After his death, it was discovered that he had willed much of his estate to former players.

"One thing people always misunderstood about Frank and Everett," Smith said, grinning. "Frank would always run over to shake hands. Everett didn't do that. He always ran to the dressing room. He said, 'We'll shake hands down below.' Frank said, 'No, I'm going to come after you and shake hands, otherwise you're running from me.'"

Like McGuire and Case, and like his rival, Mike Krzyzewski, Smith, too, had arrived in North Carolina from elsewhere. Born in 1931, he had grown up in Emporia, Kansas, then Topeka. It intrigued me how the prevailing sensibilities of Kansas and North Carolina seemed so closely matched. Each state valued the plainspoken, the modest, and the unadorned. Within that plain speech, of course, there were many ways for a man to shade his meaning, to say both more and less than was suggested by the face value of the words. Smith was a master of this. "I say what I think," he said, "just not everything I think."

If Kansas were a Southern state, it would have been North Carolina, and if North Carolina were a Midwestern state, it would have been Kansas. Both states staked out the middle as if that were the most honest place to be. Topographically, Kansas lay for the most part as flat as a pool table, and North Carolina enjoyed both mountains and coastline, but in terms of cultural geography, they were brothers. I suspected that this might be the legacy of both states' agricultural roots. That such cultures might tend towards the laconic struck me as a reasonable response to the fact that crops were rarely impressed by the fast talkers of mercantile societies. Crops needed rain, not promises.

I tried this theory out on Smith's longtime assistant and fellow Kansan, Bill Guthridge. It rapidly became clear that he had no idea what I was talking about.

In Kansas, Smith enjoyed an All-American boyhood, the son of stern, but loving schoolteacher parents. There were inklings, though, of a more complicated world. He recounted a story about himself in high school. He played quarterback on the Topeka team with a talented black receiver named Adrian King, who he remembered had once saved a game against Salina by adroitly snaring a bad pass of Smith's late in the fourth quarter, tying the score. "But they wouldn't let him play basketball," Smith said. "I went to the principal, because he was an ex-football coach who was a friend of Dad's. I said, 'You know, Adrian would really help our team. Why is it he has to play on his own team?' And the principal said, 'Dean, that was just something we decided to do because we'd have trouble with all these . . . you know, at the dances after the basketball games.' And how dumb I was, I said, 'Oh,' and walked out."

Despite his early run-ins with racial prejudice, Smith was still shocked when he came South the first time and saw a drinking fountain marked "Colored Only." In tandem with a young preacher fresh in town named Robert Seymour, the leader of the new Binkley Baptist Church, Smith set about testing the willingness of local restaurants in Chapel Hill to conform to the new law guaranteeing all races equal across businesses and public facilities.

"Chapel Hill got a reputation for liberalism from Mr. Howard Odum and the Sociology Department at the university," said Seymour, one of Smith's closest friends. "But Chapel Hill was as segregated as Mississippi. The only place in town where you could sit with a black was Danziger's, a place run by a refugee from Hitler's Germany or Austria. The former senator Frank Porter Graham said that Chapel Hill is like a lighthouse. It sends its beam into the distant darkness, but like a lighthouse, it is also dark at the base."

Smith and Seymour decided to take a black guest to the Pines Restaurant. "We were going to test them," Seymour said. "Dean had a vested interest in the Pines because the basketball team ate its pre-game meals there. Everything went smoothly. The Pines, along with other restaurants, had been castigated by people in the community for resisting reform. We turned out to be like any Southern town."

But it was in that town, my town, that Smith became a moral exemplar. I remember him in his big, pimpin' Carolina-blue Cadillac, an ocean liner of a car, nosing into a tight spot at Granville Towers during his annual summer basketball camp, at which I had managed to secure a spot through the intervention of our next-door neighbor, a donor to the athletic program. The Cadillac itself had been a gift of boosters.

Dreamer that I was, raised on sports biographies, with their morals of pluck and practice rewarded, I tried to catch Dean Smith's eye at camp. He himself had devoured the sports novels of John Tunis, having been required by his mother to read a book a week. So he knew a little about fantasies and persistence and discovery.

We were taught, as were his players, to point a finger at the passer after receiving an assist that led to our scoring. It was a lesson in giving credit to the usually unsung, deflecting praise from the overvalued act of scoring. Paradoxically (in the usual Smith fashion), this seemed a fine way to ensure that credit came back your way. Basketball camp, therefore, became a veritable orgy of finger-pointing (the good kind). When the server at the Granville Towers chow line plopped a mound of mashed potatoes on our plates, we pointed at him. We couldn't all be good players, necessarily, but we could all be good finger-pointers.

But I didn't just point my finger. I ran suicides like a G.I. trying to catch a departing helicopter. I screened and cut and passed. I eschewed the dribble. I didn't hog the ball. I knew that Smith valued teamwork above all else, that he sometimes told the story of coaching a phys-ed team at Air Force, where, as Smith put it wryly, he had a player who "shot only when he had the ball." Smith escorted the shooter's four teammates off the court. "Okay, play them by yourself," he told the gunner. "Who takes the ball out of bounds, sir?" he asked Smith. "Good," Smith told him. "Now you've learned that you need two, anyway."

I did have my suspicions, that, despite what coaches say about the value of sharing the ball, there was danger at basketball camp in being consigned to the unseen role of the hustler, like being a helpful spinster aunt in a Jane Austen novel. You ended up blending so well into the woodwork that you weren't actually seen. Better, perhaps, to shoot a lot, though if you were going to do that, better to hit the shots.

Sad to say, I don't think Dean Smith caught a glimpse of my heroic screen-setting. I did attract the notice of Bill Guthridge, but that was for whistling "Stairway to Heaven" while waiting to be subbed into a game. "Way to whistle," he said. He winked at me, patted me on the shoulder, and kept on walking.

There were times where Dean Smith's story seemed more familiar to me than my own. Though he would never admit it, it was something of a saint's tale—a saint who snuck cigarettes before games in the entryways of gymnasiums, who drank liquor and got divorced and kept a messy desk and loved winning and hated losing, and who kept score with a long memory for jibes and doubters and cheaters. "Dean never forgets anything," the journalist Bill Brill told me, "and he won't let you forget it, either." Brill recalled that when North Carolina won Smith his first national championship in 1982, Dean's first order of business in the victorious press conference was to respond to Frank Barrows, a writer for *The Charlotte Observer*, who had suggested several years before that Smith's team made such a fetish of consistency that they would never be able to achieve the peak performances necessary to win it all.

And yet, all of these qualities just made his goodness seem more plausible to us everyday sinners. There was something old-fashioned about learning morality through the example of a human being—not from books or sermons or stone tablets, but from an actual life in front of you. Someone who was grinding through the same existence we all were, and yet demonstrated the allure of goodness, who made a case for an ethical behavior rooted in compassion and fellow-feeling—not in the fear of hellfire and damnation, nor in the dictates of the Bible as the ultimate rule book, as was so common in my native South even to this day.

I asked Seymour to what he attributed Smith's decency. He thought for a moment, then said, "I attribute this to a sound upbringing in a good family. He had a family that gave him the good sense to care about others." "Value each human being," Smith's father used to tell him.

Smith extended the realm of family to his players, upon whom he exerted an abiding moral influence as a compassionate but toughminded paterfamilias. Not even Michael Jordan, whose freedom to do what he wished must have felt near-absolute during his glory days with the Chicago Bulls, who as a sporting demigod enjoyed immunity from simple necessities like waiting in line—not even Jordan could escape Smith's moral suasion. It was as if his former coach had become a voice in his head, a conscience that spoke with that nasally Kansas twang.

As recounted by David Halberstam in his biography, *Playing for Keeps*, Jordan, then a few years into his career as a Bull, arrived late for a pre-season exhibition game at Carmichael Auditorium on the UNC campus, where parking was hard to come by on the best of days. Jordan drove into the parking lot next to the gym, only to discover every space filled, except for a single handicapped spot. "Why not take it?" his friend Fred Whitfield asked.

"Oh, no, I couldn't do that," Jordan answered. "If Coach Smith ever knew I had parked in a handicapped zone, he'd make me feel terrible. I wouldn't be able to face him."

The question that Smith seemed to answer with

his life was how to compete in this dog-eat-dog society, how you competed and even won without turning into a monster. Clearly, Smith hardly minded winning. In fact, he hated to lose.

He revealed that his composure concealed powerful extremes of emotion. "Sometimes I get so upset at myself," he said, speaking in the present tense. "I don't let it show, but I'm really mad." He cited a game that happened nearly 15 years ago against Georgia Tech, in which the Yellow Jackets' Dennis Scott beat UNC at the last second with a three-pointer falling out of bounds. Smith blamed himself for not having coached a better end of the game.

"Win or lose," he said, "I go to sleep. Then I wake up the next morning and it hurts worse." He seemed relieved not to have to go through that anymore. "I don't read the paper after a loss," he added.

"So how did you learn to lose?" I asked, "It seems coaches would go insane if they didn't."

The answer, Smith suggested, lay in a notion called "the power of helplessness," a concept introduced by the writer Catherine Marshall, whom he'd come across in his thirties when reading religious thinkers like Soren Kierkegaard, Karl Barth, Dietrich Bonhoeffer, and Martin Buber, among the many suggested to him by Bob Seymour. "Crisis brings us face to face with our inadequacy," Marshall had written in a book called *Beyond Our Selves*, "and our inadequacy in turn leads us to the inexhaustible sufficiency of God. This is the power of helplessness, a principle written into the fabric of life."

Smith discovered Marshall's work the same week in 1965 that he was hanged in effigy—twice—in front of the Woollen Gym by Carolina students unhappy with the direction of the program under his leadership. A few days after the latter hanging, the Tar Heels upset sixth-ranked Duke at Cameron, 65 to 62. Invited to speak to a celebrating crowd of students outside of Woollen up the team's return, Smith declined. "I can't," he said. "There's something tight around my neck that keeps me from speaking."

He learned how to apply Marshall's lessons directly to coaching. Giving up in that context meant teaching his players to surrender to the present moment in practice and in games, not to fret about something that was beyond their control in either the future or the past. They were to let go of what they could not control. He helped them—and himself—sidestep the self-immolating demands of victory at all costs. "When we talked to our team over the years," he told me, "our emphasis was always play hard, play smart, and play together. We didn't mention winning. The emphasis was on process versus end result." Many would find it ironic that a coach famous for controlling everything he could ultimately believed in letting go. But the most important lesson of all, one that had generated decades of loyalty from his former players, was Smith's equal treatment of every player, from benchwarmers to stars. He wanted to show them that their value as human beings was separate from their performance on the court.

"The emphasis on process—was that just a sneaky way to get the result you wanted, i.e., winning?" I asked.

"You could say that," Smith said with a Mona Lisa smile. I didn't know whether the smile suggested a realization of the contradiction between not thinking about winning so that you could win, or whether it was simply an acknowledgment that coaches were in the business to win and that if they didn't, they'd shortly be in the broadcasting business. But that you might as well try to win in a dignified and decent manner. And lose that way, too.

In this part of the world, coaches were philosopher-kings, their evident wisdom on such matters as full-court pressure and team dynamics eventually translated into realms far afield; both Smith and Mike Krzyzewski had written books applying their coaching secrets to business success. Not long ago, Smith had finished his manual, called *The Carolina Way: Leadership Lessons from a Life in Coaching.* Krzyzewski had published a book entitled *Leading with the Heart: Coach K's Successful Strategies for Basketball, Business and Life.* Journalists sought their opinions on matters like the war with Iraq. Politicians asked for their help in fundraising.

And yet for all of that, one of the things I admired about Dean Smith was that the American vogue for self-promotion appeared lost on him. He didn't court publicity in a country where hype, good or bad, had become a value in its own right. I doubted he had his own blog, for instance. Or that he would be making a commercial for American Express in which he said, "I don't look at myself as a basketball coach. I look at myself as a leader who happens to coach basketball."

He inveighed against the way TV, for instance, zeroed in on the sideline antics of coaches. He had once asked a CBS executive to stop showing coaches during their college basketball broadcasts. "But it's good for the game!" the astounded executive responded.

"Too much is made of this coach-versus-coach business," Smith told me. "It's a player's game."

As for the Duke-Carolina rivalry, his initial position appeared to be: What rivalry? This was vintage Dean Smith. In time, he qualified his view.

He admitted that Duke under Vic Bubas had proved a tough opponent in the '60s. But in the latter part of that decade, Smith's program caught fire, in part when he out-recruited the Blue Devils for the high school All-American Larry Miller, a six-four bruiser from Catasauqua, Pennsylvania. "He was the big breakthrough," Smith said. "By the time he was ready to sign, Duke had a class of six committed. And Larry said, 'Gosh, I won't get any playing time on the freshman team if I go there.'" From 1967–1969, the Tar Heels won three straight ACC Tournaments at a time when only the tournament champion advanced to NCCA play. And for those same three years, UNC went to the Final Four, losing in the championship game in 1968 to UCLA and Lew Alcindor. Duke began a slow fade from sight.

The following decade, Smith said, "There wasn't really any Duke-Carolina rivalry." He thought for a moment. "The team that's beating you is the team that becomes your big rival." In the '70s, that meant North Carolina State, with David Thompson, had been Carolina's most detested foe. Then Maryland for a time. Then, in the early '80s, Virginia, with Ralph Sampson at center and Terry Holland as coach. (Holland had named his dog Dean because—as he puts it—the dog whined a lot.) "After Sampson left . . . I was trying to remember . . . Duke . . . they didn't beat us much."

And then Smith said, as if trying to recollect something lost in the recesses of either time or his mind: "Duke... I suppose they did come on about '85 or '86."

How Smithian, that "I suppose"! In a sense, Smith's reluctance to put Duke into a special category was the cagiest, most rivalrous move of all. By not considering your archrival your archrival, you were injuring him at his most vulnerable point: You refused to give him the prominence he gave you. You were saying he simply wasn't that big a deal! You were saying there was a long list of competitors of which he was one and that perhaps at certain times in the historical record, Duke may have amounted to a pretty good team. But that in the long march, Duke was as often as not standing at the curb, watching the parade go by. Masterful! Ingenious! Devious! And brilliant!

In 1985, Duke successfully out-recruited North Carolina for Danny Ferry. "When we lost Danny Ferry," he told me, "that was the start of their program." This was the same Danny Ferry whose SAT performance was to become a matter of public comment by Smith.

"John Feinstein was furious with me about that," Smith said of the Duke-educated journalist, author of *A Season on the Brink*, a rather terrifying glimpse into the mind of Bobby Knight. "He said it was the worst thing that I commented on how Reid's and Williams' SATs combined surpassed Ferry's and Laettner's. I said, 'How do you know that all of them didn't score 1400 or 1500?' Feinstein was so much of a Duke guy."

The controversy occurred the same week as the 1989 ACC Tournament finals, which, in karmically just fashion, ended up being between Duke and North Carolina. The game was a bitterly contested slugfest, bodies bouncing about the lane, every shot challenged. At one point, Krzyzewski stared down the sideline at Smith and yelled, "Fuck you," a remark that was instantly entered in the unexpurgated ledgers of the rivalry. The outcome wasn't decided until Ferry barely missed a long heave at the end of the game. The Tar Heels prevailed, 77 to 74, a win that doubtless gave Smith great satisfaction.

By the time he resigned in 1997, Smith had gone on quite a run against the Blue Devils. "I'd have to check," he said, "but I think Duke beat us once in about ten times before I retired."

"That is exactly right," I said. I knew. Those sorts of things mattered to me, too.

I had come to visit a saint of the everyday to learn about how to be good and how to lose with grace, and had discovered a coach who was still competing, sitting down there in his very own basement giving as good as he ever got—or better. Let the games continue.

Danny Ford: The Man, the God

By Michel S. Stone

Lights flickered like fireflies below my dorm window, pinpricks in the Carolina midwinter darkness. Angry cries rose, indecipherable, feverpitched, echoing among the trunks of elms and Southern magnolias.

My roommate Kelly and I pressed our ears to the cold glass.

"Oh, no, Max must go! Oh, no, Max must go!"

Kelly's eyes rounded. "They're going to President Lennon's house."

We slammed our ears to the pane again, so as not to miss another word.

"Oh, no, Max must go . . ."

"Should we join them?" I asked.

"Are you crazy?" She stared at me only a moment before squashing her nose against the glass, shielding her eyes from our room's florescent lights in a vain attempt to see Coach Danny Ford's fiercest supporters, surely anticipating the president's house doused with gasoline, a mere football field's length from where we stood.

I was a little bit in love with Coach Ford. Had been since age nine when my parents returned from Clemson's 1978 Gator Bowl victory over the once-great Woody Hayes and his Ohio State University Buckeyes. The match-up had been Ford's first as the Tigers' head coach, and ended up being Hayes's last as the Buckeyes'.

That game was the stuff of gridiron fairy tales. Danny had avenged the evil deeds of nasty, old Hayes, a Buckeye gone bad, who'd lose his job for punching Clemson linebacker Charlie Bauman in the chest after Bauman intercepted a late fourth-quarter OSU pass.

Of course I was in love with him; anyone whose blood ran orange had a thing for Danny—Danny, youngest Division I coach in the country; Danny, a product of legendary Alabama coach Paul "Bear" Bryant; Danny, the Gator Bowl champ.

Perhaps my initial affection was puppy love, but then in 1981 Danny did what no man had done before: he coached Clemson to a National Championship. After our Orange Bowl victory over Nebraska, I'd never turn back. Danny . . . Was . . . The . . . One.

"Danny is the Man," I said to the girls gathering in my room.

I'd traveled to the Citrus and Gator Bowls the previous two years. Like the mob below us, I knew the deal.

Earlier that day, as my friend Elizabeth and I made our way across campus from Fike Recreation Center to Smith dorm, we passed a sports reporter from my hometown of Charleston. I had no doubt why he was on campus.

"Warren Pepper!" I shouted. Maybe I was a bit in love with him, too. He'd been on television since I was a kid.

"Hey, there," he said.

"I'm from Charleston," I said, by way of introduction. "You here because of Coach Ford?"

"We are," he said, nodding to a cameraman beside him. "Mind if I ask you a few questions?"

The cameraman raised his big, black lens.

"Okay." I giggled at Elizabeth, who was from Rock Hill, and therefore oblivious to the magnitude of Warren Pepper's presence.

"What's your reaction to Coach Ford's resignation?"

Leaning toward the microphone, I waxed eloquent. "Well, it's Danny Ford, you know? I'm shocked, just really shocked." I added a profound, "Danny is the Man," for good measure.

I called my parents as soon as I hit my dorm room. "Be sure to watch my interview," I said.

Months earlier, during my sophomore year, I'd stopped for coffee at the Hardees on my walk to class. Danny Ford stood at a register. Right there. Beside me. I was 19 and had watched him on the sidelines for 10 years, but I'd never seen him up close. He had pockmarked skin and dark, intense eyes, raccoon-like in their beadiness, just absolutely wonderful. He ordered a biscuit to go.

I'd called my parents that day, too. "Guess . . . who . . . was . . . right . . . beside . . . me . . ."

Stories have at least two sides. Some have more. The common thread to the rumors was that the administration had done Danny wrong. Many believed that the university had sold Ford down the river in return for a lighter sentence from the NCAA (we were in the midst of yet another investigation for recruiting violations). Who knew? Who cared?

This was, after all, Danny.

Juicier rumors swirled about a player's involvement with one of Ford's daughters. Who could be certain? The reasons didn't matter; our young king had been dethroned, his subjects enraged. The student body united against the administration. We had no great cause to rally around in the late 1980's like our predecessors in the 60's and 70's. Perhaps we at Clemson were ripe for a cause, and ours was discovered in trying to resurrect the career of Danny Ford.

The evening of the rally, players and fans gathered on Bowman Field, and state troopers assembled for crowd control. Students attending reported a palpable craziness, a sense of danger. Some had packed coolers of beer, and went just to watch the action, but the rage that overtook the crowd dumbfounded them. Several of Ford's players proclaimed through bullhorns they'd not play another game for Clemson if Ford were not reinstated.

And then someone shouted, "Let's get Max!" and the tumult building on Bowman Field opened up, unable to contain itself, and rolled through East Campus, past my dorm window toward President Max Lennon's house.

The mob could do anything if they fueled their rage with action, if they approached Lennon's house, refusing to leave until he surfaced, relented, raised his hands in defeat and said, "O.K., O.K., he may stay. Ford will remain our football coach."

But President Lennon did not surface, and he did not say those words.

That was 1990, yet the die-hards hold out hope still. (One only has to Google Coach Ford today—nearly two decades later—to find the site DANNYISGOD.) His followers, in the words of another ACC great (although Jim Valvano was a hoops coach in North Carolina), "Don't ever give up."

The following year, during homecoming, I played the role of Clemson's new coach Ken Hatfield in my sorority's skit for Tigerama. A running joke in our skit was Hatfield's big ears. My friend Marcella had penned the skit, and I asked her later, after we'd been named first runners-up, "Does Hatfield really have big ears?"

"I have no idea," she shrugged.

I didn't know either. But I knew Danny's mug like a photo before my eyes.

Danny was the Man.

Coach K

By Jim Sumner

We all know what they say about hindsight being 20/20. Some things seem so inevitable, so logical that we cannot imagine them turning out differently. Duke University basketball coach Mike Krzyzewski falls into that category. In his twenty-ninth season in Durham, Krzyzewski has become an icon, hugely successful on the court, a go-to person for almost any issue impacting college basketball, a sought-after speaker, an author, the CEO of a nationally-recognized behemoth. How could it have been otherwise?

But there was a time when such success at Duke seemed uncertain, even unlikely, a time when the young, embattled Krzyzewski seemed to be immersed in waters well over his head.

The Duke program wasn't exactly in trouble when Krzyzewski arrived in the spring of 1980. Bill Foster had revived the program after a period of dormancy. Duke finished second in the 1978 NCAA Tournament and advanced to the Mideast Region final in 1980.

But Foster was always more interested in building a program than in sustaining one. So when South Carolina approached Foster to replace the retiring Frank McGuire, Foster said goodbye to Durham, finishing the season as a lame duck.

Duke Athletic Director Tom Butters had a number of plausible options to replace Foster. The in-house candidate was 30-year-old Bob Wenzel, Foster's top assistant and a recognized up-and-comer in the profession. Hiring Wenzel would enable Duke to maintain program continuity.

A more experienced possibility was Paul Webb, head coach at Old Dominion and former head coach at Randolph-Macon. Webb had been coaching college basketball since the 1950s.

In between was Bob Weltlich, who had just completed his fourth season as head coach at the University of Mississippi. Younger than Webb, more experienced than Wenzel.

Wenzel, Webb, and Weltlich. One Durham sportswriter was so certain that they comprised the short list that he assured his readers that Duke's next coach would answer to Coach W. He was wrong. Flying so far under the radar that he wasn't mentioned by any media was Mike Krzyzewski.

A native of Chicago, Krzyzewski attended the United States Military Academy, where he started for the basketball team coached by Bob Knight. Krzyzewski graduated from Army in 1969 and spent five years in the Army, much of it coaching service teams.

By the time Krzyzewski left the military, Knight was head coach at Indiana University. Krzyzewski spent one year there assisting Knight, before becoming head coach at Army for the 1975–'76 season.

With high academic standards, military discipline, and a five-year service commitment waiting, the military schools do not generally attract high-school recruits with NBA aspirations. Not a likely place to start a hall-of-fame coaching career. But Army defied the odds twice, once with Knight and then with Krzyzewski.

Krzyzewski led Army to the National Invitational Tournament in 1978, about the highest rung realistically available for the school. But a young Army team went 9–17 in 1980, bringing Krzyzewski's record there to 73–59.

Butters says he was looking for "the finest young defensive coach in the country, someone who understood what Duke was about, and someone who could beat Dean Smith, because if you could beat North Carolina, you could beat anyone."

Steve Vacendak was Krzyzewski's point-of-entry to Duke. Vacendak was a star guard at Duke in the 1960s and in 1980 had just started as the assistant athletic director at his alma mater.

But Vacendak had spent some time in the late 1970s in Annapolis, Maryland, representing Converse. He managed an invitation to an Army practice prior to an Army-Navy game. "I was impressed," remembers Vacendak. "He was organized, his practice was well thought-out. I knew that anyone coaching successfully at Army had to use every X and O they had. You weren't going to beat people any other way."

Vacendak mentioned Krzyzewski to Butters, who was receptive. Butters was more than receptive after talking to Knight, an old friend just four years removed from winning his first NCAA title at Indiana.

Butters remembers, "Bob told me if I liked him as a defensive coach, then I would like Mike. So that got my attention. Then he told me that Mike had all of his good qualities and none of his bad qualities."

Krzyzewski came in for an interview and then a follow-up in Lexington, Kentucky, where Duke was playing in the NCAA Tournament. Butters says, "Mike impressed me as a coach and even more as a person. He was everything that I was looking for. But I couldn't pull the trigger. I couldn't get over that 9–17 record at Army."

Vacendak adds, "Mike was bright, articulate, and passionate. He could communicate and we thought he had the discipline and self-control to forge through adversity. Mike has that ability to get people on board. He doesn't impose his will as much as he gets people to buy into something in such a way that they feel invested in it and feel a part of it."

Butters brought the Final Four candidates back for one final interview, with Krzyzewski last. The Army coach was on his way back to the airport when Butters decided there was no point in mulling over the decision any longer. He sent Vacendak out with the instruction not to let Krzyzewski get on that plane. "You're not going to interview him again?" asked Vacendak. "No, I'm going to hire him," responded Butters.

Butters was leader of a committee, but a committee that gave him wide latitude on this hiring. He formally offered the job to Krzyzewski and the acceptance was instant. Butters recalls mentioning to Krzyzewski that they had not discussed salary. "Whatever you decide," Krzyzewski said. "I know you'll be fair."

Krzyzewski's hiring took everyone by surprise. The school newspaper, the *Duke Chronicle*, ran the headline "Krzyzewski: This is Not a Typo." Guard Vince Taylor says, "I had never heard of him, never heard him mentioned. I was stunned."

It's tempting to see this as Woodward and Bernstein meeting Deep Throat in a deserted parking garage. But Butters and Vacendak insist that there was no special effort to keep Krzyzewski's name from the public. "People latched onto the obvious names," says Vacendak. "Mike wasn't an obvious name. They didn't do their homework."

Kenny Dennard was a rising senior at Duke. He had been recruited by Foster and had started three seasons for Foster. Dennard was in Key West when the news broke. "This was before ESPN, before the internet. It was like Pony Express. I saw something in *USA Today* and thought, 'hmm.'"

Krzyzewski was 33 when he moved to Durham, barely a decade older than his most-seasoned players. Dennard says, "We didn't know who he was, what he was going to do. We were more curious than anything else."

There were some changes, the biggest concerning defense. Foster was a master at using multiple defenses. Dennard says, "We changed defenses all the time. We might use one defense when the other team had the ball at halfcourt, another for a full-court defense, then switch when they got the ball past halfcourt. It was a big part of who we were."

Krzyzewski would have none of that. Knight was a disciple of the man-to-man defense and Krzyzewski was a disciple of Knight, at least in this area. For Krzyzewski, a man-to-man defense was a way that a basketball team imposed its will on the opposition: aggressive, confrontational, in-your-face.

More than anything else, Krzyzewski's reliance on the man-to-man defense would become his program's signature. Clemson coach Bill Foster (not the same Bill Foster who coached at Duke) once observed that Duke started guarding you as soon as they got off the bus.

But if Krzyzewski had areas in which he would not compromise, he was quite flexible in other areas. Dennard notes, "People sometimes are surprised to hear this, but he was very patient. He was a teacher. If the effort was there, he would work with you over and over. But the effort had to be there. He wanted you to be the best you could be but he didn't try to turn you into somebody you weren't."

Duke went 17–13 in 1981, defeating North Carolina in the home finale, and advancing to the third round of the NIT. Not quite at the recent level but a qualified success.

But storm clouds were on the horizon. The team's best players were Dennard and fellow senior Gene Banks, and Taylor, a junior in 1981. Foster didn't leave Krzyzewski much else. The cupboard was getting bare and Krzyzewski knew he had to bring in some players from the high-school class of 1981 who could come in and play right away.

He came agonizingly close. A half-dozen of the nation's top prep players came down to Duke and another school. All picked the other school: Chris Mullin and Bill Wennington to St. John's, Uwe Blab to Indiana, Jimmy Miller to Virginia, Wayne Carlander to Southern California, Rodney Williams to Florida.

Duke did sign Dan Meagher, a tough forward from Ontario, and three fall-backs.

The results were predictably dire. The 1982 Duke team was the worst in modern Duke history—small, slow, lacking depth, ball-handling, shooting.

So bad that Krzyzewski frequently abandoned his beloved man-to-man defense for a zone, just to keep the score close. Duke eked out a 10–17 record, largely on the heroics of Taylor, who led the ACC in scoring.

Some of the losses were excruciating. Krzyzewski's team lost to Appalachian State. At home. Maryland beat Duke in Cameron Indoor Stadium, 40–36, a game in which not one Duke point was scored by a player taller than 6-feet-5-inches.

Duke ended its season with a 35-point loss to Wake Forest in the ACC Tournament. A mercy killing, in most opinions.

But Krzyzewski was winning those recruiting battles he had lost the year before. Convinced that he had overextended himself, he concentrated on a narrower range of targets, prioritizing earlier and making a few key prospects the focus of his efforts.

Krzyzewski had Duke to sell, he had the ACC to sell. But most of all, he had that rare ability to conceive, articulate, and sell a vision.

California native Jay Bilas was one of the key recruits who turned around Duke basketball. Now a basketball analyst for ESPN, Bilas recalls, "I honestly didn't know where Duke was. He (Krzyzewski) explained how he would build the program, how we would win. I trusted him. It's as simple as that. He was honest, straightforward, and never wavered. I wanted to play for him."

The key recruit was guard Johnny Dawkins, a stunning talent from Washington, D.C. Dawkins was the kind of recruit college coaches salivated over, the kind of recruit that Krzyzewski had to sign to be able to compete in the ACC. The kind of recruit who didn't go to schools coming off 17-loss seasons.

But Dawkins committed to Duke only days after that dispiriting loss to Wake Forest. Dawkins also cites Krzyzewski. "He did such a great job of recruiting me as an individual, painting a vision for my future. He was fiery, competitive, and knew where he wanted to go and how to take us there."

Krzyzewski calls Dawkins "our first legitimate big-time recruit. He could win the tough games we had not been winning."

Dawkins inspired Mark Alarie, another prep All-American, to decide to come all the way from Arizona to Duke. David Henderson, from tiny Drewry, North Carolina, was the sixth and last recruit in what would become the most significant recruiting class in Duke basketball history.

Krzyzewski had his team. But the college basketball universe was a different place in 1983. Some top college players would go to the NBA with eligibility left. James Worthy led UNC to the 1982 NCAA title as a junior and left for the pros. But Ralph Sampson, Virginia's 7-foot-4-inch center, returned for his senior season in 1983 after being selected national player of the year in 1981 and 1982. And he was typical. Top teams were dominated by juniors and seniors. It was a dangerous neighborhood for freshmen.

Duke still had a trio of seniors, leftovers from the Foster regime. One, guard Chip Engelland, averaged more than 15 points per game in 1982 and was one of the best outside shooters in the ACC. Doug McNeely was the lone junior and there were four sophomores.

The logical course of action was to blend in the

freshmen gradually, mixing and matching them with their veteran teammates, playing zone, trying to minimize mistakes.

But Krzyzewski knew that his program would rise or fall with this class and he figured he might as well throw caution to the wind. Alarie says that the freshmen were "thrown into the deep end of the pool to see if we could swim."

The freshmen played often and early. Four of the top five in minutes played that season were freshmen, an astonishing statistic. And they played man-to-man. Krzyzewski says, "We had a plan and were going to stick with it. Defense was going to be our foundation. It would have been foolish to wait."

But the cliché "growing pains" doesn't begin to describe the difficulties of the learning curve. The freshmen struggled together and learned together. The program reached a nadir on January 5 when Duke lost at home to tiny and unheralded Wagner College, 84–77.

This was the last straw for some influential supporters. A few years earlier Butters had started the Iron Dukes, an athletic support group. A handful of high-rollers calling themselves the Concerned Iron Dukes demanded Krzyzewski's dismissal and they were quite forceful in their demands. Butters says, "They wanted Mike gone and they wanted him gone now. If I wasn't going to fire him, then they wanted me gone."

But Butters had the strong support of school president Terry Sanford, a former North Carolina governor who wasn't about to be intimidated by the Concerned Iron Dukes.

Butters' support for Krzyzewski was equally strong. "Everything I had seen convinced me that I had made the right choice," says Butters. "He had the system in place, he was getting the players he needed, and the program was heading in the right direction. All that was needed was some patience." Vacendak adds, "The more we saw of Mike, the more we were convinced that we had made the right choice. There was no Eureka moment, just a process, but a process with a clear result."

The remainder of the 1983 season was a rollercoaster ride. Duke traveled to College Park and stunned Maryland 10 days after the Wagner loss. Two more ACC wins followed.

But Duke suffered another shellacking in the ACC Tournament, a 109–66 loss to Sampson and Virginia. This remains the largest margin of defeat in Duke history. Following the loss, the coaching staff and some support staff went out for a late meal. A member of the Sports Information staff glumly proposed the toast, "Here's to forgetting tonight." The defiant Krzyzewski interrupted, "No, here's to never forgetting tonight."

Duke didn't forget. Dawkins, Alarie, and company never lost again to Virginia. In fact, Duke followed that 1983 loss with 16 consecutive wins against Virginia.

Of course, by that point, Duke was beating a lot of people. The callow freshmen of 1983 grew up. Duke advanced to the NCAA Tournament in 1984 and won an NCAA-record 37 games in 1986 before losing the NCAA title game to Louisville in the dying seconds. Krzyzewski replaced Dawkins and Alarie with more high school All-Americans, winning three NCAA titles and establishing a dynasty that continues to this day.

Butters is retired now but still follows Duke basketball with a justified pride. "Mike's a great basketball coach but he'll never be as good a basketball coach as he is a person. In fact, I don't think of him as a coach. He's an academician, a counselor, someone who cares about the kids who play for him as much as we care about our kids."

And none of this would have happened if Tom Butters and Duke University hadn't rolled the dice on a virtual unknown back in 1980 and trusted their choice long enough to see it pay off in ways they scarcely imagined.

Born to Coach, Summerville Legend John McKissick Not About to Stop

By Rob Young

To say he is a man of convention would be an understatement of colossal measure.

For the past 15 years, coach John McKissick, head of the wildly successful Summerville [High School] football program, has essentially eaten the same breakfast: grapefruit, bowl of cereal with strawberries, bananas and peaches, "when they're in season." He eats nearly the same meal for lunch, a bowl of yogurt with strawberries, bananas and peaches, again when they're in season.

Now 81, he has held the same job for 56 of those years. He and his wife have lived in the same home for 53 years, just a mile or two from the high school, and a few streets over from Halcyon Road.

In that time he has kept winning—convention can be a beautiful thing—amassing 556 victories and 10 state championships. No. 11, he hopes, comes today when his team travels to Columbia, facing Byrnes in the Division I-AAAA title game. A victory today would give McKissick state championships in six different decades.

John Updike wrote the tragedy in being a teacher—for what else is a coach but a teacher—is that they remember so many students, though so few remember them.

It doesn't apply to McKissick, the winner of more games than any other high school football coach in the nation. So many remember.

"Summerville as a town has changed tremendously over the years," says Bo Blanton, one of McKissick's former quarterbacks. "But football on Friday nights in Summerville has remained the one constant, and that one constant is really John McKissick."

The phrase, "My blood runneth green," is etched in cross-stitch and hanging in the McKissicks' trophy room—their Green Wave room—a trove of keepsakes and plaques and pictures, dozens of scrapbooks, all chronicling McKissick's career.

McKissick's wife/historian, Joan, has documented her husband's life and records since the beginning, since the blood turned green when they came to Summerville.

"It was just a little village then," Mrs. McKissick says. "All the streets were dirt streets. Just [Highway] 17 coming through town was about the only paved street. Everybody came to the post office to get mail. Everybody knew everybody."

McKissick's shadow was slight, the unproven 25-year-old coach taking the reins from a legend,

Originally published in The Charleston Post and Courier, *December 2007.*

Harvey Kirkland, who secured a pair of state championships in 1948–49 and football's hold on the town. McKissick won his first state title in 1955 and his second crown came in '56, two years before Byrnes coach Chris Miller was born.

McKissick remembers when he started, Summerville had 296 students in the top four grades.

"I was the coach," McKissick says. "I did football, girls basketball, boys basketball, baseball. I added track. I don't know how in the world I did it."

Now, the high school has roughly 3,400 students. McKissick, himself, has 10 coaches on the football staff.

And as the school has grown, so has Summerville. In the early days, he'd drive around town in an old pick-up he bought from surplus in Columbia, and stop by the pool hall, poke his head in, to make sure all his boys were home by 9:00.

He'd make them get haircuts if they wanted to play. He still hates long hair, and ear bobs, he really hates ear bobs.

"He calls them ear bobs sometimes because that's what they called them growing up," Mrs. McKissick says.

"But all their heroes wear them," McKissick says. "So we let them wear 'em around the school, just not on the field."

Adaptation has been his ally. First rule of convention: Choose the practical solution. The best systems require retrofitting.

"He's been able to adapt better than anyone I've ever seen, especially as a coach," says Billy Long, one of McKissick's former players and coaches. "The kids have changed, and it's not just football. It's everything."

But it's a strange thing, really, as Mrs. McKissick notes, to have your disposition, fortune and happiness dictated by 17- and 18- year-old boys.

"Sometimes they just plain mess up and make mistakes and errors that they don't always make," she says. "We don't hold it against them because that's life. You accept it."

But the losses still sting, now perhaps more than before. Summerville's only defeat this season came in the season opener, a 36–3 thumping from Booker T. Washington, a heavyweight program out of Florida, the game televised on ESPN.

"He was so disappointed," Mrs. McKissick says of her husband. "He was really embarrassed. That was humiliating for him because he thought we were a lot better than we were."

Those losses have been few, the program only suffering two losing seasons under McKissick, one in 1957, the other in 2001. And to think, he never seriously considered another job, through the years rejecting offers from his alma mater, Presbyterian College, The Citadel and Newberry College.

"When I wake up in the morning, I'm so glad I never tried to leave," he says. "There's not a better place to live than here."

Retirement, it seems, is fodder for another season. He feels young, and looks younger than his age, wearing a pair of stylish bifocal frames. Already, he has said he'd like to return.

"It just scares him to think about it," Mrs. McKissick says. "He just does not like to talk about it or think about it because he cannot picture his life. When you've done something for 56 years, it's hard to imagine what in the world you're going to do when you hang it up."

Life becomes much shorter as you get older. McKissick has said as much before. Might as well keep at it.

"At the best, I ain't got many more years," he says, "and I don't want to sit around and think like that. So, that's why I stay busy. I've got a lot of buddies who retired, started out when I started out, and they're already dead."

Still, after the years, the wins—and it bears repeating—10 state championships, why keep going? What's left to prove?

"The one this year," he says.

"When life kicks you, let it kick you forward": The Life and Impact of Kay Yow

By Susan Shackelford

It was 1974, and Kay Yow agreed to coach an all-star team of top collegiate women's basketball players, most of whom were from North Carolina. Sound like fun? Well, maybe.

Consider that the opponent was an all-star team from the country that dominated international play in women's basketball at the time, the Soviet Union. The U.S. women had not beaten the Soviets for 17 years. And they didn't this time, losing by a whopping 114–41 at Elon College, where Yow coached the women's basketball team.

The Soviets rebounded and sprinted past the Americans as if they were sleepwalking, impressing Yow and the approximately 4,000 spectators in Alumni Gymnasium. "Their fast break was awesome," Yow said after the game. "We didn't think they would be as fast or as quick. We had planned to use the running game ourselves as much as we could, but as it turned out, we were defending against their break."

The Soviets' seven-foot star, Uljana Semjonova, who eventually would be enshrined in the Naismith Memorial Basketball Hall of Fame, played only the second half and scored 10 points. Her team didn't really need her that Monday evening in May. It led 53–13 at halftime.

The key to the Soviets' success was simple: They were tall—eight of their 13 players were over six feet, compared to only three of the Americans. But more importantly, the Soviets worked together like gears of a finely tuned machine. They had played together for years and years, something rare among their American counterparts.

In fact, women's basketball teams in the U.S. were fairly rare at the time. This was pre-Title IX, when the game was episodic at best in the Carolinas and the rest of the country. It was only through coaches like Yow, a Gibsonville, North Carolina, native, that the game spread quickly once Title IX, a federal law, required that schools provide sports opportunities for girls and women.

Yow went on to a stellar career as the women's basketball coach at N.C. State and as a part of U.S. international teams. The U.S. Olympic team she coached in 1988 in Seoul, Korea, won the gold medal. She led N.C. State to the Final Four in 1998 and is sixth among women's collegiate basketball coaches in career wins (737 victories). In 2002, she became only the fifth female coach to be inducted into the Naismith Memorial Basketball Hall of Fame.

But Yow became known for more than just her

basketball accomplishments. She succumbed at age 66 to a long battle with breast cancer, which in the latter stages had spread to her liver and bones. Along the way, she inspired people with her positive outlook and steely resolve to overcome the disease. One of her favorite expressions was, "When life kicks you, let it kick you forward." She refused to feel sorry for herself.

"I don't think, Why me?" she told *The New York Times* in March 2006. "I think, Why not me? I don't think anything. It's life. And as you go through life, it's just, to me, inevitable that you're going to face tough times."

Yow was first diagnosed with breast cancer in August 1987, 11 months before she was to coach the Olympic team in Seoul. She underwent a modified radical mastectomy and soon became active in raising money to fight the disease.

Yow learned in November 2004—a little over 17 years since her initial diagnosis—that the cancer had returned. She underwent surgery again, missing two games during the 2004–05 season.

Two years later, the disease had spread to her liver, and she missed 16 games during the 2006–07 season. She returned late in the season to inspire her team to a major upset of unbeaten and No. 1-ranked Duke in the semi-finals of the Atlantic Coast Conference Tournament and to a Sweet-16 finish in the NCAA Tournament.

She began the 2008–09 season but missed four games early on. After that, she took a leave of absence for the season and entered the hospital to try, once again, to make a comeback. She died peacefully in her sleep on Saturday, January 24, 2009. Her courageous battle touched people far and wide.

"Kay never allowed herself to be victimized by cancer," Tennessee Coach Pat Summitt said. "Kay never pitied herself. Instead, she tried to bring awareness to the horrible disease that was robbing her of her life. Through . . . the Kay Yow/ Women's Basketball Coaches Association Cancer Fund, in partnership with The V Foundation for Cancer Research, she did all that she could do to help others. That was just Kay."

Yow's passion for others and her knack for basketball made her an outstanding coach and pioneer of the modern women's game.

Born March 14, 1942, Yow came from a basketball family. Her parents, Hilton and Lib Yow, played on high school and textile mill teams. Her cousin Virgil coached the three-time Amateur Athletic Union champion Hanes Hosiery Girls, as well as men's teams at Hanes and High Point College.

Hilton and Lib erected a basketball goal in their backyard when their oldest child, Sandra Kay, turned seven.

By the time Kay reached high school in the mid-50s, the state girls' high school tournament had been eliminated, but she lived in a community where local support for women's basketball still ran strong.

Starring at Gibsonville High School, she routinely played in front of packed gyms, once scoring 52 points in a game. She earned her team's most valuable player honor all four years of high school and made the state's East-West all-star team her senior year.

Yet in 1960, when Yow graduated second in her class, the future coaching star took the same route as most of her high school peers—she quit the sport.

Without a protest, without a whimper.

She went to East Carolina Teachers College to

become an English teacher and librarian. The school didn't even have a women's basketball team. "It was very different then, like everything else," Yow said decades later. "I grew up in a time where people answered questions. They didn't ask questions."

But the irony is, when she sought a job after college, it was her basketball talent that snared it.

She applied for a job teaching English at Allen Jay High School in High Point, N.C., not far from her family in Gibsonville. Principal Doyle Early knew of her basketball skill and offered her a deal: coach the girls' team and she could have a teaching position. Yow accepted and quickly became a success. Her first team went 22–3 and won the conference title. Her next two teams also won conference titles.

After four seasons at Allen Jay, she coached her sister Susan Yow and her Gibsonville High team for two seasons. Kay then started the women's basketball team at nearby Elon College in 1971. Her sisters Susan and Debbie played for her there, and Kay amassed a 57–19 record and two state championships over four seasons.

On July 1, 1975, N.C. State Athletic Director Willis Casey hired her not only to coach basketball but to build a women's athletics program in the wake of Title IX. She served as the women's sports coordinator and coached volleyball and softball as well.

Her sister Susan transferred to N.C. State and became an All-American basketball player at the Raleigh school. After graduation, Susan, too, went into coaching and is currently the coach at Belmont Abbey College in Belmont, N.C. Debbie also became a coach. She then moved into college sports administration and fundraising, and today is the athletic director at the University of Maryland.

In Kay's 34 years as N.C. State's women's basketball coach, she led the Wolfpack to 20 NCAA tournaments and 11 Sweet 16s. She is one of only three coaches to coach 1,000 or more games at one institution. (Her record was 680–325 at N.C. State and 737–344 overall.) The others are former Texas coach Jody Conradt and Tennessee coach Pat Summitt, two other icons of the modern women's game.

In preparation for the 1984 Olympics, Summitt asked Yow—10 years her senior—to serve as her top assistant coach.

"Kay had great wisdom," Summitt recalled. "She had a special way of telling you things that you really didn't want to hear but needed to. Kay was not a 'yes' woman. She accepted the challenge of helping me to bring home the first gold medal to the United States in women's basketball. It was a daunting task, but Kay made it so much easier by helping to relieve the pressure."

Yow's rapport with players was vital. "I learned so much from her on how to better communicate with your players," Summitt continued. "She definitely always knew the pulse of our team and had a calmness about her that was so settling to me as a young coach."

Two years later, Yow earned her own place in the international spotlight. Remember that drubbing her all-star team took in 1974 against the Soviet Union? Well, it was payback time.

In preparation for being the U.S. Olympic coach in 1988, Yow coached the first-ever U.S. women's team in the Goodwill Games in the summer of 1986. She also coached the U.S. women's team in the World Championships the same summer. Both events were in Moscow, and both times the Americans beat the Soviets and won the events. Yow's teams broke a nearly three-decades-old dominance that the Soviet Union had had over American women's teams.

Then Yow's 1988 Olympic team defeated the Soviet Union in the semi-finals in Seoul, en route to beating Yugoslavia for the gold medal.

Since that lopsided loss in 1974, Title IX had vaulted Yow to coveted coaching positions at N.C. State and on the international level. It also fueled a big leap in the caliber of play by American women. Who better to shepherd such momentous changes than Yow, a leader who inspired both on and off the court.

"What an impact Kay had on so many," said Atlantic Coast Conference Commissioner John Swofford. "Whether one of her players, an opposing coach, a friend, an associate in the world of sports or one who observed her grace, dignity, elegance, kindness and competitive spirit from a distance, you couldn't but be touched by her presence in our world."

Acknowledgments

I would like to thank all of the contributors to this book for sharing their stories of sports in the Carolinas, especially Jerry Bledsoe, Will Blythe, Dick Brown, Ron Green, Sr., Clint Johnson, Sharyn McCrumb, Lenox Rawlings, Susan Shackleford, Tom Sorensen, and Rob Young. I would also like to thank the many editors—including Julie Harris at the *Winston-Salem Journal*, Rick Thames at the *Charlotte Observer*, Margaret Williams at *Mountain Xpress*, and the editors of the *Charleston Post & Courier*—who granted us permission to use previously published stories.

Stephen Kirk deserves particular thanks and credit for coming through spectacularly on short notice.

Thanks to Jamie Rogers, Carolyn Sakowski, and Drew Southern, for suggesting story ideas and possible contributors, and for helping me shape my own contributions to this anthology.

Most of all, I would like to thank Amy Rogers and Betsy Thorpe at Novello Festival Press, for giving me this opportunity.

List of Contributors

Jerry Bledsoe is the author of 22 books. His work has appeared in numerous publications and anthologies. He lives in Randolph County, N.C.

Will Blythe is the author of *To Hate Like This Is To Be Happy Forever* (HarperCollins). For many years, he served as the literary editor of *Esquire* magazine. He edited *Why I Write* (Little Brown), a collection of essays. He grew up in Chapel Hill and lives in New York City.

Betty Brown is primarily a studio/*plein air* artist and art teacher who enjoys writing. She is intrigued by relationships between word and image. Journaling on painting trips often triggers poems and stories. A finalist in the Randall Jarrell Poetry Contest while studying at UNC-W, her work was published in *Atlantis*.

Dick Brown was raised in Spencer, N.C., but spent most of his career as a graphic artist and supervisor for Raytheon in Greenville, Texas. After early retirement he built a second career as a journalist at several newspapers in Texas. He now lives in Winston-Salem with his wife, Penny.

Ann Campanella is proud to be the sister of a Special Olympian. Formerly a magazine and newspaper editor, she writes poetry and creative nonfiction. Her latest poetry collection, *Young & Ripe*, (Main Street Rag) was published in March of 2009.

David C. Dickson was born in Texas but has spent most of his life in Surry County, N.C. Dickson's fiction and poetry have been published in the *North Carolina Literary Review, Asheville Poetry Review,* and featured in the *Raleigh News and Observer Sunday Reader.* Dickson is a high school history teacher, and the father of two sons.

Clarence E. "Big House" Gaines, who is enshrined in seven halls of fame, was elected to the Naismith Memorial Basketball Hall of Fame in 1982. Coach Gaines died in April, 2005, but is remembered with the highest esteem by the basketball community and by everyone who knew him, worked with him and played for him.

Ron Green, Sr., covered sports for the *Charlotte News* and *Charlotte Observer* for more than 50 years. He has been inducted into five halls of fame, including the North Carolina Journalism Hall of Fame. He is also the author of six books.

Jack Igelman's articles about the outdoors have appeared in many magazines and newspapers and he is the co-author of *Trekking the Southern Appalachians* (Mountaineers Books, 2005), a backpacking guidebook. A former Outward Bound instructor, he lives in Asheville, N.C.

CLINT JOHNSON writes in Ashe County, N.C. He learned of Coach "Big House" Gaines' style of blunt honesty when Coach asked of the intermediary who introduced them (after Clint had left): "Where'd you find that nitwit?" It was the start of a warm friendship. See all his books at www.ClintJohnsonbooks.com.

KRIS JOHNSON is an assistant managing editor at *NASCAR Scene* and a contributor to both *NASCAR Scene* and *NASCAR Illustrated*. His debut novel, *The Endgame*, was published in 2002.

STEPHEN KIRK is the editor at John F. Blair, Publisher, and the author of *Scribblers: Stalking the Authors of Appalachia* and *First in Flight: The Wright Brothers in North Carolina*. His fiction has appeared in the *Best American Short Stories* series. He lives near Winston-Salem, N.C.

MICHAEL KRUSE, a 2000 graduate of Davidson College, is a staff writer at the *St. Petersburg Times* in Florida. His work also has appeared on ESPN.com, and in the *Sporting News, ESPN The Magazine* and *Charlotte* magazine. His first book, *Taking the Shot: The Davidson Basketball Moment*, came out in late 2008.

SHARYN MCCRUMB, a *New York Times* best-selling author, won a 2006 Library of Virginia Award and the AWA Book of the Year Award for *St. Dale*, honoring NASCAR's Dale Earnhardt. Best known for her "Ballad" novels, set in North Carolina's mountains, McCrumb was named a 2008 *Virginia Woman of History*.

MATT MUSSON was born in Texas and lives in N.C., where he develops software for Bank of America and works part-time for the Charlotte Bobcats. He writes for boys and his first novel, *The 51 Rocks: Batboy on the Worst Team Ever*, is under contract to Baker Tritten Press.

LENOX RAWLINGS first met Mary Garber when he covered sports for the *Raleigh News & Observer* while still a student at UNC-Chapel Hill. He became "Miss Mary's" colleague when he came to work for the *Winston-Salem Journal*, after stints with the *Greensboro Daily News* and the *Atlanta Constitution*. He has been a sports columnist for the *Winston-Salem Journal* since 1978.

MICHAEL SCOTT was a graduate business student at Duke during its 1989 ACC-championship season (yes, in football). He is an aspiring polymath masquerading as an insurance executive. Mike lives in Winston Salem, N.C., with his wife Julie and four children. This is his first published work.

SUSAN SHACKELFORD is a Charlotte-based writer and former full-time sports writer for the *Charlotte Observer* and the *Miami Herald*. She co-authored *Shattering the Glass: The Remarkable History of Women's Basketball* with historian and fellow Charlotte-based writer, Dr. Pamela Grundy.

TOM SORENSEN grew up in Minneapolis (as did Ric Flair), and majored in journalism at the University of Minnesota. He came to Charlotte in 1981, and has been a sports columnist for the *Charlotte Observer* since 1985. He says about his love for pro wrestling, "Sports used to be the great escape. Rasslin' still is. That isn't real life in and around the ring; it's louder and more brash. There's more spandex and hair dye. It collects interesting people."

ED SOUTHERN is the Executive Director of the N.C. Writers' Network, as well as the editor of *Sports in the Carolinas, Voices of the American Revolution in the Carolinas*, and *The Jamestown Adventure*. His debut work of fiction, *Parlous Angels*, will be published in September 2009 by Press53.

MICHEL S. STONE has published about a dozen short stories. A native of Johns Island, South Carolina, she now resides in Spartanburg with her husband Eliot and their three children. She recently completed her first novel, *The Crossing*, and is hard at work on her second one. She remains an avid fan of all things Clemson.

Raleigh-based writer **Jim Sumner** is the author of numerous books and articles on southern sports history. A graduate of Duke University and North Carolina State University, Sumner is a columnist for theacc.com, *Blue Devil Weekly* magazine, and *Inside Carolina* magazine. His latest book is *Tales From the Duke Blue Devils Hardwood*.

R.G. (Hank) Utley, after retirement in 1998, researched and wrote (edited by Scott Verner) *The Independent Carolina Baseball League, 1936–1938* and *Outlaw Ballplayers* (edited by Tim Peeler) in 2006. Both were published by McFarland and were named History Book of the Year by the N.C. Society of Historians.

Rob Young is a features writer for the *Charleston Post & Courier* in Charleston, S.C.

This is a continuation of the copyright page

"A Triumph for Title IX" copyright © 1994 by Susan Shackleford; first published in the *Charlotte Observer*; reprinted with permission.

"Big House, Billy, and the Unofficial Integration of Winston-Salem" copyright © 2004 by Clint Johnson and Clarence E. Gaines and excerpted from *They Call Me Big House*, published by John F. Blair, Publisher; used with permission.

"Born to Coach, Summerville Legend John McKissick Not About to Stop" copyright © 2007 by Rob Young; first published in the *Charleston Post and Courier*, December, 2007; reprinted with permission.

"Choo Choo" copyright © 2003 by Ron Green, Sr.; originally published in the *Charlotte Observer*, October 18, 2003; reprinted with permission.

"Mary Garber Stood Very Tall in a Man's World" copyright © 2008 by Lenox Rawlings; first published in the *Winston-Salem Journal*, September 22, 2008; reprinted with permission.

"Mountaineers Bring Down the House" excerpted from *King of the Mountain: The Jerry Moore Story* copyright © 2008 by Dick Brown and published by John F. Blair, Publisher; used with permission.

"Nose Dive" copyright © 2006 by Jack Igelman, first published in *Mountain Xpress*, Asheville, N.C., on October 4, 2006; reprinted with permission.

"Ryan Newman's Canine Connection" copyright © 2008 by Kris Johnson; first published in *NASCAR Scene*, February 28, 2008; reprinted with permission.

"The Coach in the Basement": pages 49–62 from *To Hate Like This is To Be Happy Forever* by Will Blythe; copyright © 2006 by Will Blythe. Reprinted by permission of HarperCollins Publishers.

"The Outlaw Carolina League, 1936–1938" copyright © 1999 and 2006 by R.G. (Hank) Utley; adapted from *The Independent Carolina Baseball League, 1936–1938* by R.G. (Hank) Utley with Scott Verner; and *Outlaw Ballplayers* by R.G. (Hank) Utley with Tim Peeler; both published by McFarland; used by permission of the author.

"The World's Number One, Flat-Out, All-Time Greatest Driver: Richard Petty" copyright © 1975, 1976, 1995 by Jerry Bledsoe; first published in the *New York Times*, 1975. Excerpted from *The World's Number One, Flat-Out, All-Time Great Stock Car Racing Book* and reprinted with permission from Down Home Press.

Index

#3: The Dale Earnhardt Story 112
ACC Tournament 40, 86, 123
Alarie, Mark 138–139
Ali, Muhammad 99–101
"All the Way, Choo Choo" 74
American Basketball Association 86–87
Appalachian State University Mountaineers 49–53
Atlantic Coast Conference 13, 26, 39, 56–60, 105, 144–147

Bailey, Thurl 39–41
Barrows, Frank 128
Baseball Hall of Fame 71–72
"Battle of the Palmetto State" 12
Bauman, Charlie 132
BB&T Field 58, 60
Bilas, Jay 138
"Black Sox" *see* Chicago White Sox
Blanton, Bo 141
Blue Devils *see* Duke University
Blue Ridge Parkway 15–16
Bogues, Tyrone "Muggsy" 46–47
Boone, Daniel 75
Boston Red Sox 69–70
Bowden, Tommy 14
Brian's Song 56
Brill, Bill 128
Brind'Amour, Rod 65–66
Browning, Wilt 37
Bryant, Paul "Bear" 132
Bubas, Vic 130

Bull Durham 17
Burleson, Tommy 85
Butters, Tom 136–140
Byrnes, James 13

Cameron Indoor Stadium 138–140
Capers, Dom 62
"Cardiac Pack" *see* N.C. State University
Carmichael Auditorium 19, 106, 128
Carolina Hurricanes 64–66
Carolina League 5–6
Carolina Panthers 61–63
Carr, Lloyd 50–51
Carruth, Rae 62
Case, Everett 125–126
Central Intercollegiate Athletic Association 43–45
Chaisson, Steve 65
Chappell, Len 43–45
Charles, Lorenzo 39–41
Charlotte Bobcats 114–115
Charlotte Coliseum 46–48
Charlotte Hornets 46–48
Chicago Bulls 113–115
Chicago White Sox 71–72
Childress, Randolph 57
Childress, Richard 109–112
Choo Choo: The Charlie Justice Story 74
Clay, Cassius *see* Muhammad Ali
Clemson University Tigers 12, 132–134
"Coach K" *see* Mike Krzyzewski
Cobb, Charlie 49

Collins, Kerry 61–62
Curry, Stephen 21, 22, 26, 29–31, 33, 87

Dale 112
Dale Earnhardt Incorporated 110–112
Davidson College Wildcats 21–34
Davis, Baron 48
Davis, Eric 62
Davis, Lawrence "Crash" 6
Davis, Stephen 62
Davis, Walter 105–106
Dawkins, Johnny 138–139
"Dean Dome" *see* Dean E. Smith Center
Dean E. Smith Center (Dean Dome) 19, 125
"Death Valley" *see* Memorial Stadium
Delhomme, Jake 61–63
Demon Deacons *see* Wake Forest University
Dennard, Kenny 137
Denver Nuggets 86–87
Dorrance, Anson 54–55
Drexler, Clyde 39–41
Driesell, Charles "Lefty" 23, 45, 86
Duke University Blue Devils 10, 135–140
Duncan, Tim 56–57
Durham Athletic Park 17
Durham Bulls 17
Durham Bulls Athletic Park 18

Earnhardt, Dale 107–112
Earnhardt, Dale Jr. 107, 108, 110–112

Earnhardt, Ralph   107–108
Earnhardt, Teresa   110–112
Easter Monday baseball games   3–4
Edwards, Armanti   49–53
Eight Men Out   72
Elder, Jake   109
Ernie Shore Field   69–70
Erving, Julius   87
Ferry, Danny   131

Field of Dreams   71
Flair, Ric   102–104
Ford, Danny   132–134
Ford, Phil   123
Foster, Bill   135, 137
Fox, John   61–63
Francis, Ron   64–66
Frazier, Joe   99–101
Futch, Eddie   99–100

Gagne, Verne   102
Gaines, Clarence E. "Big House"   42–45
Gamecocks *see* University of South Carolina
Gannon, Terry   39–41
Gantt, Harvey   114
Garber, Mary   81–84
Gilbert, Sean   62
Gillespie, Bob   15
Grand National Circuit *see* NASCAR
Granite Falls Graniteers *see* Granite Rocks
Granite Rocks   37–38
Greene, Kevin   62
Greensboro Coliseum   64
Grobe, Jim   57–60
Groves Stadium *see* BB&T Field
Guthridge, Bill   126, 128

Hamm, Mia   54–55
Hampton, Wade   13
Hartford Whalers   64
Harvick, Kevin   111–112
Hatfield, Ken   134
Hayes, Woody   132
Heisman Trophy   14, 74
Heisman, John   14
Helms, Jesse   114
Henderson, David   138
Hill, Cleo   43–45

"The Hive" *see* Charlotte Coliseum
Hogan, Hulk   104
Holtz, Lou   14

Inman, Dale   90, 109
"Iron Dukes"   10

Jackson, "Shoeless" Joe   71–72
Jackson, Dexter   52–53
James, LeBron   29
Jenkins, Kris   62
"Jimmy V" *see* Jim Valvano
Johnson, Larry   47
Johnson, Robert Glenn "Junior"   75–76, 92
Jordan, Michael   40, 47, 54, 103, 113–115, 124, 128
Justice, Charlie "Choo Choo"   73–75

Karmanos, Peter   64
Kasay, John   61–62
Knight, Bob   135–137
Krzyzewski, Mike   39, 123, 125–126, 130–131, 135–140

Landis, Kennesaw Mountain   71
Lane, Fred   62
Laviolette, Peter   65–66
Lennon, Max   132–134
Long, Billy   142
Longenecker, Steve   15
Looking Glass Dome   15–16
Lowe, Sidney   39–41
Lucas, Ken   63
Lynch, Corey   51–52

Mack, Connie   72
Major League Baseball   71–72
Maurice, Paul   65
McCormack, Mark   80
McGuire, Frank   123, 125
McKillop, Bob   21–34
McKinney, Horace "Bones"   44–45
McKissick, Joan   141–143
McKissick, John   141–143
McLendon, John   42
McQueen, Cozell   39–41
Memorial Stadium (Death Valley)   12, 62

Miller, Larry   130
Mills, Sam   61–62
Minter, Mike   62
Monroe, Earl   42
Moore, Jerry   49–53
Moore, Margaret   49–53
Morgan, Dan   62
Mountaineers *see* Appalachian State University
Mourning, Alonzo   47
Muhammad, Muhsin   62

N.C. A&M *see* N.C. State University
N.C. Central University   42
N.C. College for Negroes *see* N.C. Central University
N.C. State University Wolfpack   3, 39–41, 85–86, 144–147
Nantz, Jim   39
NASCAR   75–76, 91–98, 107–112, 118–120
National Association of Professional Baseball Leagues   5
National Basketball Association   86–87, 113–115
National Football League   61–63
National Hockey League   64
National Wrestling Alliance   102–103
NCAA Men's Basketball Tournament   21, 39–41, 86, 135–140
Newman, Ryan   118–120
Nicklaus, Jack   80
"The Nose"   15–16

Ohio State University Buckeyes   132
Olajuwon, Akeem   39–40
Osterlund, Rod   108–109

Packer, Billy   43–45, 56
Packer, Mark   56
Palmer, Arnold   56, 80
Parsons, Benny   97–98
Paul, Chris   56–57
Pearl Harbor   10
Pearson, David   88, 109
Peppers, Julius   62
Pepper, Warren   133
Petty, Lee   88–92
Petty, Maurice   88, 91

Petty, Richard   88–98, 109
"Phi Slamma Jamma"   39
Phills, Bobby   47
Piccolo, Brian   56
Pinehurst No. 2   8–9
Pinehurst, N.C.   7
Pisgah National Forest   15
Pit Road Pets   119
Player, Gary   80
Primeau, Keith   64
Proehl, Ricky   63

Queens College   78–79

Rauch, Julian   52
Rice, Glen   47
Richard Childress Racing   109–112
Richards, Jason   22, 27–28, 30–33
Richardson, Jerry   61–63
Richardson, Kevin   50–53
Roberts, Fireball   88
Robinson, Jackie   82
Rogers, George   14
Rose Bowl   10–12
Ross, Donald   7–9
Rucker, Mike   62
Ruth, Babe   69–70
Ryan Newman Foundation   118–120

Sanford, Terry   139
Seifert, George   62
Shelton, Ron   17
Shinn, George   46–48
Shoeless Joe   72
Shore, Ernie   69–70
Skinner, Riley   58–60
Sloan, Norm   85–86
Smith, Charlotte   19
Smith, Dean   39, 106, 113, 123–131, 136
Smith, Steve   62–63
Southeastern Conference   13, 26
Southern Conference   10, 25, 34
Special Olympics   116–117
Springsteen, Bruce   75, 125
Sprint Cup *see* NASCAR
Summerville (S.C.) High School   141–143
Summitt, Pat   145
Super Bowl   61–63

Swofford, John   147
Tar Heels *see* University of North Carolina
Testaverde, Vinny   63
They Call Me Big House   43

Thomas, Isiah   114–115
Thompson, David   85–87
Thurmond, Strom   13
Tigers *see* Clemson University
Tillman, "Pitchfork" Ben   13
Title IX   19
Towe, Monty   85
Trinity College *see* Duke University
Tripucka, Kelly   46
Tufts, James   7–8
Turner, Curtis   88

Unitas, Johnny   61
University of California at Los Angeles Bruins   85–86
University of Houston Cougars   39–41
University of Kansas Jayhawks   21
University of Michigan Wolverines   49–53
University of North Carolina Tar Heels   11, 54–55, 73–74, 105–106, 113, 123–131
University of South Carolina Gamecocks   12
Updike, John   141

Valvano, Jim   39–41, 125

Wade, Wallace   10
Wake Forest College *see* Wake Forest University
Wake Forest University Demon Deacons   3, 23, 43–45, 56–60, 80
Walls, Wesley   62
Walton, Bill   86
Waltrip, Darrell   75, 109
Waltrip, Michael   111–112
Ward, Cam   65–66
Washington Redskins   74
Watts, Bob   15
Wellman, Ron   60
Wesley, David   48
Western Carolina League,   37–38

Whitehurst, Charlie   14
Whittenburg, Dereck   39–41
Wildcats *see* Davidson College
Williams, DeAngelo   63
Williams, Roy   54
Williams-Bryce Stadium   13
Winston Cup *see* NASCAR
Winston-Salem State University Rams   42–45
Winston-Salem Teachers College *see* Winston-Salem State University
Wolfe, Tom   75
Wolfpack *see* N.C. State University
Wolverines *see* University of Michigan
Wooden, John   85
Woods, Tiger   80
Worsham, Bud   80

Yarborough, Cale   75, 97–98, 109
Yow, Debbie   146
Yow, Kay   144–147
Yow, Susan   146

NOVELLO FESTIVAL PRESS

Novello Festival Press, under the auspices of the Public Library of Charlotte and Mecklenburg County and through the publication of books of literary excellence, enhances the awareness of the literary arts, helps discover and nurture new literary talent, celebrates the rich diversity of the human experience, and expands the opportunities for writers and readers from within our community and its surrounding geographic region.

THE PUBLIC LIBRARY OF CHARLOTTE AND MECKLENBURG COUNTY

For more than a century, the Public Library of Charlotte and Mecklenburg County has provided essential community service and outreach to the citizens of the Charlotte area. Today, it is one of the premier libraries in the country—named "Library of the Year" and "Library of the Future" in the 1990s—with 24 branches, 1.6 million volumes, 20,000 videos and DVDs, 9,000 maps and 8,000 compact discs. The Library also sponsors a number of community-based programs, from the award-winning Novello Festival of Reading, a celebration that accentuates the fun of reading and learning, to branch programs for young people and adults. The Library was a winner of the 2006 National Awards for Museum and Library Service, the nation's highest honor for libraries and museums that make their communities better places to live.